A SATIRE
OF THE THREE ESTATES

A Satire of
The Three Estates

by

SIR DAVID LINDSAY

A play adapted by
Matthew McDiarmid
from the acting text made by
Robert Kemp
for
Tyrone Guthrie's
production at the Edinburgh
Festival 1948 with music by
Cedric Thorpe-Davie

Introduction and Notes by
Matthew McDiarmid

Theatre Arts Books
New York

Introduction and Notes © Matthew P. McDiarmid 1967

This version first published 1967

Library of Congress Catalog Card No. 67–28050

Published by
Theatre Arts Books
333 Sixth Avenue, New York 10014
Printed and Bound in Great Britain by
Bookprint Limited, Crawley, Sussex

CONTENTS

INTRODUCTION

The Author

Sir David Lindsay was born in 1486 on his father's estate, the Mount, in Monimail parish, Fife, the county which contained the metropolitan seat of the Scottish Church, St Andrews, and where the movement for ecclesiastical reform was strongest. Where he received his education is not known, but before 1511 a place had been found for him at the court. In that year, the Treasurer's Accounts tell us, he performed in an interlude at Holyrood Abbey, wearing a 'play-coit' of blue and yellow taffeta. After the king's death in the battle of Flodden (1513) he was appointed gentleman-usher to the infant James V, a post which he lost with the coming to power of the Earl of Angus in 1524 and regained with the young king's escape from the earl's tutelage four years later.

It seems to have been his experience in these years of government by a self-seeking faction that made him commence as a poet and satirist, for his first and best poems, *The Dreme*, his *Complaint* and *The Papyngo*, were written at this time and make all the criticisms of the nation's state that were to be voiced more extremely and powerfully in his play.

From 1530 he was one of the king's heralds and about 1542 received his knighthood and appointment as chief herald, Lyon King of Arms, in which capacity he went on various embassies – to the Emperor Charles V at Brussels, to Francis I at Paris, to Henry VIII at London and to the King of Denmark. As a herald he had the opportunity to develop the remarkable sense of dramatic spectacle that is displayed in the *Satire*: one of his duties was to supervise the pageants and other formal entertainments of the court, and he is known to have composed the masque which welcomed the newly arrived queen, Marie de Lorraine, to St Andrews in 1538. It seems likely also that the first version of the

Satire, played before the king and queen in Linlithgow Palace on Twelfth Night 1540, was occasioned by James's temporary wish to conciliate England and the Scots party of reform. The daring of its political and ecclesiastical criticisms and their reported acceptableness to the king can hardly be explained otherwise.

James's motives, however, do not reflect any ambiguity in Lindsay's reforming attitude. This was soon displayed in the most partisan way. Provoked by English aggression the government soon reverted to an anti-reform policy, which was not halted by the rout of Solway Moss and the king's consequent death (1542) but intensified under the direction of Cardinal Beaton. When the cardinal was assassinated in 1546 in his castle at St Andrews, where two months earlier he had watched the burning of George Wishart for heresy, Lindsay published his detestation of the dead man in a poetical 'tragedie' and visited the murderers in the seized castle. Only such considerations as his personal prestige and the government's need to temporize in a threatening situation can have allowed him to retain his official post. In 1552 he presented his play in a much expanded and much more trenchant form at the Castle Hill of Cupar in Fife, and in 1554 it was performed at Edinburgh before the Queen-Regent herself. Lindsay died in the following year.

His final theological position, Protestant or Roman Catholic, is still a matter of debate. His contempt for the hierarchy of his day is not. His approach to the issues of reform was indeed not so much that of the theologian as the practical moralist, and his criticism was not aimed only at the Church as such but at 'Covetice' as practised by all three of the governing Estates. His subject was justice in the commonwealth, and it may be said that his moral concern is less with the private than the public relations of men. That he was no Puritan, in the common sense of that term, is evidenced not only by his play but also by the delightfully human account that he wrote, only two years before, of the love affair of a deceased friend, William Meldrum – he had too lively a sense of humour and too realistic an appreciation of the appeal of Lady Sensuality.

The Text

A Satire of the Three Estates is known to us from three sources: an eye-witness's detailed report of the Linlithgow version of 6 January 1540; George Bannatyne's transcript of 'only Sertane mirry Interludes thairof', derived from the Cupar play of 7 June 1552; and Robert Charteris's 1602 edition, which reflects its performance on the Greenside at Edinburgh, 12 August 1554. The two texts that concern the editor do not differ significantly where they can be compared. The edition shows lengthening of a few lines and some unimportant verbal changes but no serious attempt at revision – Douglas Hamer's statement that the character of the Prioress has been introduced overlooks the testimony of his own comparative texts (vol. 2, p. 132). It is necessarily Charteris's Quarto that is mainly followed in the present text, but the evident interference of Anglicizing printers in some instances has encouraged the present editor to prefer some of the earlier readings.

What is published here is not everything that Lindsay wrote but, with some additions that will be noted, the inspired selection of lines made by Robert Kemp for Tyrone Guthrie's celebrated Edinburgh Festival production of 1948, which discovered the dramatic merits of this liveliest and most interesting of pre-Elizabethan dramas. Their selection omitted very little in the action or speeches of the *Satire* that was essential to the significance or effect intended by Lindsay. His own Edinburgh production, according to Charteris, lasted nine hours, and though very lengthy intervals are obviously included in this reckoning, the total text represents a duration of entertainment that few modern audiences would find acceptable. Considerable cuts therefore were required, yet it was possible to make them in the way described. The mere repetitiousness and comparative irrelevance of some of the matter that so prolonged a spectacle imposed upon its provider, could be cut without much loss of meaning – thus the unactable obscenity of the Pardoner's devil's ceremony of divorce between a cobbler and his wife (referred to in my note to. l. 1498), that delighted an idling crowd between serious

9

scenes, was left out; as also a somewhat lengthy model sermon, and a recital of proposed Acts of Parliament that had already been implicitly or explicitly recommended in the play; the part of Common Theft; and finally the *sermon joyeux* of Folly, which concluded the performance by farcically rehearsing criticisms already made.

This last excision has been accepted, though it helps to clarify an aspect of Lindsay's conception of the action that should be clear enough elsewhere but has been generally overlooked by critics. The editor has departed, however, from the Festival arrangement in certain instances[1] – in allowing Theft to come on and be hanged, since the Border reiver's farewell speech appeared too significant a part of Lindsay's social panorama to be omitted; in letting Covetice make his momentary but meaningful appearance; in giving something more of the comic interlude of Chastity and the Craftsmen, a little more of the Pardoner's scene, and a few more of the absurdly self-revealing speeches of the members of Spirituality.

The major change has been a scrupulous return to the words of Lindsay – except for the half-dozen cases where 'if' has been substituted for 'gif' and 'to' for 'till'. Since this text is intended, however, for the student of literature and not phonology, the spelling has often been brought nearer to the more familiar one of later Scots poetry, though usually in such a way as to render Lindsay's sounds approximately.

The stage directions of the Festival producers, which reflect Lindsay's intentions and often merely amplify his own, have been retained in italics, as also the two sixteenth-century Scots songs which appropriately supplied the ones missing from the extant texts. Difficult words are glossed for the reader's convenience, while the longer notes will provide the fuller comprehension of the text needed by students.

[1] Lines inserted by the editor are indicated by the initial M in the notes on pages facing the text.

The worthwhile result of this editorial procedure is that Lindsay's masterpiece is presented in an acting version that speaks only his language and gives a just idea of his dramatic intention and achievement.[2]

Commentary

Dunbar and Lindsay both mention the 'farses and plesand plays' enacted at the Scots court but these have not come down to us, and the three lonely descriptions of plays previous to the *Satire* are not of court productions. One is of a Passion play, composed in 1535 by a Friar John Kyllour, for a Perth audience, that is said by John Knox to have sharply criticized the religious hierarchy; the others, with the same intention, are a tragedy of 'John the Baptist' and a comedy of 'Dionysius the Tyrant', written by James Wedderburn and acted about 1540 at the West Port and play-field of Dundee. Their agreement with Lindsay's play in respect of purpose and out-of-doors staging illustrates the peculiarly propagandist and popular turn that Scots drama had taken in these years. The *Satire* is thus very much a play 'of the people and for the people', a fact that accounts for much of its abounding vigour. How much it benefited from this popular address is made clear when it is compared with the very different form that it took at its first production in Linlithgow Palace. The comparison indeed provides the best means of appreciating the peculiar nature and quality of Lindsay's dramatic achievement.

The Twelfth Night interlude of 1540 was more or less correctly so described by its reporter. It was a simple 'morality' piece with conventional comic elements, presenting ten characters – Solace, the merry Prologue; a king flattered by three courtiers, Placebo,

[2] For further study readers are referred to the useful editions of Douglas Hamer, *The Works of Sir David Lindsay* (Scottish Text Society, 4 vols., 1931–6), and James Kinsley, *Ane Satyre of the Thrie Estaits* (Cassell & Co., Ltd., 1954); also to the historic accounts of the Edinburgh production given by Tyrone Guthrie and Robert Kemp in their prefaces to Kemp's version, *The Satire of The Three Estates* (William Heinemann Ltd, 1951). For Kemp's Scots version see *The Scots Review*, 1948.

Pickthank and Flattery; a Poor Man who complained of being beggared by the courtiers, of suffering from the exactions of Church law and custom, of the lechery of priests, and who reminded his royal auditor that 'all erthely kings are but officers'; a learned Doctor, Experience, who confirmed the allegations of Poor Man, exposed the scandalous behaviour of nuns, and discoursed on the true office of a bishop; a Man of Arms, representing the nobility, who combined with a Burgess to support Poor Man against a wrathful Bishop who threatened him with death; the whole discourse being concluded by the apparently hitherto silent king's approving the proposed reforms. This dramatic sermon seems to have been preached with Sir David's characteristic vigour, for the Scots eye-witness asserted that after the performance James threatened to send his bishops to his less tolerant uncle in England if they did not mend their ways. Its limited cast and want of action, however, must have precluded any hint of the panoramic vitality, the range of entertainment and criticism, that was exhibited at the Castle Hill of Cupar to an audience of Fifeshire lairds, farmers, townsmen, and their women-folk. Specifically the reader of the *Satire* will reflect how much better qualified as a Prologue is the herald, Diligence – a rôle possibly taken by Lindsay himself; how slight a part is given to the first play-king; how much life came in with the three Vices; how much more significant a conception is John the Commonweal than Poor Man, who is none the less allowed to stay and make his memorable speech; how comparatively lonely and ineffectual a representative of Spirituality the wrathful Bishop of the first version must have been; and finally, though the reader may not feel that he would greatly have missed the good sisters Chastity and Verity – Chastity's comic plight is another matter – he will certainly welcome the splendid figure of Lady Sensuality.

Also, the later play is not only more various in its characters and scenes; it presents a developing moral action in two Parts or movements, successively set in court and parliament – though there is, of course, only one setting, the stage of Lindsay's imagination, where very uncourtly and very unparliamentary figures present themselves without any effect of incongruity or interruption.

In Part I young King Humanity, as Diligence has foretold, sleeps in the arms of Lady Sensuality till Divine Correction rouses him rudely to his duty of reform. He has been led there by wanton courtiers, and now it is the opportunity of the three Vices (fools) Flattery, Deceit and Falset, to introduce misrule. The first of them is a kind of comic devil who flatters the fool in every man. He sees to it that grey-bearded Good Counsel does not come near the king, helps Sensuality to ward off Chastity, and persuades the Spirituality to accuse Verity (True Religion) of being a heretic. But now Divine Correction enters and the Vices flee, Flattery and Sensuality to the protection of Spirituality. They will be sought out and exposed there by the parliament that is now summoned.

In Part II Diligence is about to make his proclamation when he is interrupted by the complaints of Poor Man, beggared by the seizure of his mare and cows. Flattery, now a friar and pardoner, tries to sell him remission of his pains in the next world but what Poor Man wants is his livelihood in this one. Flattery is chased off but returns with the other Vices when the Three Estates enter 'gangand backwart'. Spirituality is dismayed by the king's intention of reform, still more so by the sudden appearance of John the Commonweal, who identifies the Vices, so that they are arrested, along with Lady Sensuality and Covetice. Its members have now to listen to John's charges of injustice and corruption. When a counter-charge of heresy fails, they are investigated and found to be fools. Only the indestructible Flattery escapes punishment, characteristically by helping to hang his mates. He ends the play's action with a gleeful remembrance of how

> I beguilet all the Three Estates
> With my hypocrisy.

How inadequate as a description of the play any such outline of the argument must be, the reader, still more the auditor, will easily discover. It is the auditor who will soonest learn how extravagantly vital are these morality characters, or rather caricatures, and how impressively human a spectacle this formal extravaganza presents. He will best appreciate how central are the rôles of Lady Sensuality and Flattery, how much the king of the first part and the Spirituality of the second are their puppets and fools. It is indeed a play of fools. Too much has been made of its religious and propagandist meaning. That it has such a meaning is undeniable, as undeniable as the social and spiritual abuses of which Lindsay complained. In that respect he says only what the orthodox chroniclers, men like John Mair, John Bellenden and the Franciscan, Adam Abel, had already said; it is the vehemence of his anti-clericalism – his Protestantism is arguable – that distinguishes his attack. As has been remarked, he was more the critic of a corrupt commonwealth than of an established religion and, as we shall see, his attitude was not simply that of the indignant moralist.

Beyond the theme of reform is Lindsay's other theme, one traditional to the 'sottie' or fool-play, that the number of fools is infinite and of folly there is no end: Lady Sensuality is always attractive, flattery of the self is endless, and therefore so also are error and injustice; and all these have their unfailing, tragi-comic source in humanity. It is this imaginative awareness of an essentially foolish world that one must yet try to reform into some shape of dignity, that makes Lindsay's play something more than a smart piece of Reformist propaganda. Since it is great folly and not great villainy that he exposes he gives to each object of attack a farcical vitality and human significance that frees the *Satire* from the flat and factual categories of the morality drama. Critical neglect of his real intention and consequent misunderstanding of his achievement, even when Tyrone Guthrie's performance had discovered it so brilliantly, is perhaps due to a mistaken notion that such an interpretation pertained only to the production; yet it is clear enough in Lindsay's text, and particularly in the 'sermon joyeux' of Folly – perhaps unactable nowadays and necessarily omitted in this edition – that he tacked onto his play as a kind of epilogue-commentary.

The problem of making a single story of his panoramic vision of folly gleefully disrupting a divinely ordered society was solved by Lindsay in the way that we have seen. The lively presence on the stage of the Three Estates for the greater part of the action, and the continued activity of Lady Sensuality and especially the three Vices in both Parts, secured the necessary impression of unity. The feeling for the stage that Guthrie discovered everywhere in Lindsay made him keep up a lively alternation of the grave and the gay in his action and talk. Perhaps the most remarkable single evidence of his dramatic flare, however, is the effectiveness of his many verse-forms as a means of expressing his theme. There is a variety of this sort in *Everyman* and indeed in all the moralities and miracle plays, but the *Satire* is a metrical medley. Grave stanzaic patterns, varying with the effect intended, express the aspect of order, as in the opening invocation of Diligence and young King Humanity's prayer for guidance, or parody the antiorder, as in Lady Sensuality's splendid self-advertisement; while several kinds of quick-moving patterns convey the absurdity of Spirituality and the Vices – Flattery bounds onto the stage with a clatter of rhyme and the Prioress declares for freedom and marriage in verse that sounds like a jig. The two main differences of effect are something like that between the stately pavane and the brisk French 'brawl' mentioned in the play.

This technique of various formality gives a very simple but impressive emphasis to the significant contrasts; the serious becomes the ceremoniously serious and the foolery is that of the professional fool. The opposites of Reason and Unreason are thus mutually enhanced. It is these extreme contrasts that create the extraordinary life of the play – as between the fantastic triviality of Flattery's salesmanship as a Pardoner and the distressing matter-of-factness of Poor Man's 'speech of the black verity'. Burns's *Jolly Beggars* achieves its 'life-and-go' by somewhat similar means. A play with such a theme and such a technique is perhaps best appreciated in the terms of paradox; it is one of the most brilliant examples of our serious theatre of the absurd.

MATTHEW P. MCDIARMID

DRAMATIS PERSONAE

DILIGENCE, a herald

KING HUMANITY

WANTONNESS ⎫

PLACEBO ⎬ courtiers

SOLACE ⎭

LADY SENSUALITY

HAMELINESS ⎫ her maidens

DANGER ⎭

FUND-JONET, a bawd

GOOD COUNSEL

FLATTERY ⎫

FALSET ⎬ vices

DECEIT ⎭

VERITY True Religion

BISHOP

ABBOT

CHASTITY

PRIORESS

PARSON

LORD

MERCHANT

SOUTAR, cobbler

TAILOR

JENNIE, the Tailor's daughter

SOUTAR'S WIFE

TAILOR'S WIFE

VARLET

DIVINE CORRECTION

POOR MAN

WILKIN, the Pardoner's boy

JOHN THE COMMONWEAL

FIRST SERGEANT

SECOND SERGEANT

COVETICE

SCRIBE

THEFT *or* COMMON THEFT

1–13	Stanzaic arrangement and alliterative cadence are generally characteristic of the introductions to the miracle plays and are here used for formal effect.
4	*bales*, pains.
6	*haily*, holy.
8	*seasit*, seated.
11	*shawn*, shown.
12	'Sovereigns' or 'Sirs' were common modes of addressing the more important, seated members of an audience.
14	*tent*, heed; *coy*, quiet.
14–44	announce the coming of Divine Correction and the summoning of a parliament of reform, though this will not take place till the 'sleepand' years of King Humanity, that occasioned 'misrule', have been illustrated in Part I.
17	*the whilk*, who.
18	*but variance*, truly.
24	*rung*, reigned; *thir*, these.
25	*innocents . . . beirs*. David Straton and Norman Gourlay in 1534 and George Wishart in 1546 had been burned for heresy. In Lindsay's eyes they were not heretics.

PART ONE

There is a fanfare of trumpets and the members of the THREE
ESTATES *of the Realm of Scotland enter. They are the* SPIRITU-
ALITY *or Bishops, the* TEMPORALITY *or Barons and the*
BURGESSES, *who are Merchants. They make their way on to the*
stage through the audience.

DILIGENCE: The Father, founder of faith and felicity,
That your fashion formit to his similitude;
And his Son, your Saviour, shield in necessity,
That bocht you from bales, ransonit on the Rood,
Re-pledgand his prisoners with his heart-blude;
The Haily Gaist, governor and grounder of grace,
Of wisdom and weilfare baith fountain and flude,
Save you all that I see seasit in this place,   •

   And shield you from sin,
And with His Spreit you inspire   10
Til I have shawn my desire!
Silence, Sovereigns, I require,
   For now I begin!

People, tak tent to me, and hauld you coy!
Here am I sent to you, a messenger,
From a noble and richt redoubtit Roy,
The whilk has been absent this mony a year,
Wha bade me shaw to you, but variance,
That he intends amang you to compear,
With a triumphant awful ordinance,   20
With croun and sword and sceptre in his hand,
Tempert with mercy when penitence appears.
Howbeit that he lang time has been sleepand,
Where-through misrule has rung thir mony years,
And innocents been brocht upon their biers

31   *The Three Estatis.* The ecclesiastical hierarchy, the nobility,
      the burgh representatives, made a full sitting of the Scots
      parliament; the burgesses were chiefly consulted on matters
      of finance and property, but it is less the actual functioning
      of parliament than the representative classes of the country
      that Lindsay has in mind, hence the later appearance of John
      the Commonweal and Poor Man.

51   *ane*, one.

By false reporters of this natioun,
Thocht young oppressors at the elder leirs
Be now well sure of reformatioun! (*A fanfare.*)
And here by open proclamatioun,
I warn in name of his magnificence   30
The Three Estatis of this natioun,
That they compear with debtful diligence
And to his Grace mak their obedience.
And first I warn the Sprituality,
And see the Burgess spare not for expense,
But speed them here with Temporality!
As DILIGENCE *names them,* SPIRITUALITY, TEMPORALITY
and the MERCHANTS *take their places.* DILIGENCE *turns to the
audience again.*
Als I beseek you, famous auditors,
Conveent into this congregatioun,
To be patient the space of certain hours,
Till ye have heard our short narratioun.   40
And als we mak you supplicatioun
That no man tak our words into disdain,
Howbeit ye hear by lamentatioun,
The Common-Weal richt piteously complain.
Prudent people, I pray you all,
Tak no man grief in special;
For we sall speak in general,
    For pastime and for play.
Therefore, till all our rhymes be rung,
And our mis-tonit sangs be sung,   50
Let every man keep weill ane tongue,
    And every woman tway!
A Fanfare and March. Young KING HUMANITY *enters with his
train, chief among whom are two lighthearted courtiers,* WANTON-
NESS *and* PLACEBO. *The* ESTATES *sing* '*Salve, rex humanitatis.*'
The KING *kneels before his throne.*
KING: O Lord of lords, and King of kingis all,
    Omnipotent of power, Prince but peer,

21

55   *ringand*, reigning.

57   *heaven . . . clear.* The Ptolemaic cosmography as described in
        the contemporary *Complaynte of Scotland* included a celestial
        region or heaven containing the planetary spheres, and an
        elementary or sublunar one composed of four elements,
        earth, water, air, fire.

68   *thy pleasure.* The theme of Part I is King Humanity's failure
        to prefer God's pleasure or will to his own.

70   *gars*, causes; *sic*, such.

74   *ocht*, aught.
75   *ban*, curse.

77   *Placebo*, Latin, 'I will be pleasing'; the name of the flattering
        friend in Chaucer's *Merchant's Tale*, who encourages the
        amorous inclinations of old January.

84   *rout*, company.

87   *the Mess*, the Mass

89   *shent*, undone.

22

Eterne, ringand in gloir celestial,
Unmade Maker, wha havand na matteir,
Made heaven and earth, fire, air and water clear,
Send me thy grace with peace perpetual,
That I may rule my realm to thy pleaseir,
Syne bring my saul to joy angelical.   60
I thee requeist, wha rent was on the Rood,
Me to defend from deedis of defame,
That my people report of me but good,
And be my safeguard baith from sin and shame.
I knaw my days endures but as a dream;
Therefore, O Lord, I heartly thee exhort,
To give me grace to use my diadeam
To thy pleasure and to my great comfort.
The KING takes his seat on the throne.
WANTONNESS: My Sovereign Lord and Prince but peer,
What gars you mak sic dreary cheer?   70
Be blithe sa lang as ye are here,
    And pass time with pleasure:
For as lang lives the merry man
As the sorry, for ocht he can.
His banes full sair, sir, sall I ban
    That does you displeasure.
Sa lang as Placebo and I
Remains into your company,
Your grace sall live richt merrily,
    Of this have ye na doubt!   80
Sa lang as ye have us in cure,
Your grace, sir, sall want na pleasure:
Were Solace here, I you assure,
    He wald rejoice this rout!
PLACEBO: Good brother mine, where is Solace,
    The mirror of all merriness?
I have great marvel, by the Mess,
    He tarryis sa lang.
Bide he away, we are but shent!

23

ferly, wonder.

99   *berial*, jewel.
100   *preclair*, loveliest.

104   *fleyit*, frightened.
105   *thrang*, crowd.

111   *quart*, quart-pot.
113   *nippit*, scant.
113–20 M. (see Introduction, page 11).
114   *hippit*, hipped, bodied.

117   *thocht*, though.
118   *preen*, pin.
119   *Peebles On The Green*, a poem sometimes attributed to James I, but in fact dating from no earlier than the close of the fifteenth century. Solace's hope of reward for services is as absurd as the ridiculous events of the rustic celebration at Peebles that the poem describes.

122   *sirs* (see note to 12), addressed to the audience.

I ferly how he fra us went.   90
I trow he has impediment
    That lettis him nocht gang.
WANTONNESS: I left Solace, that same great loon,
    Drinkand into the borough's toun –
    It will cost him half of a croun
        Althocht he had na mair!
    And als he said he wald gang see
    Fair Lady Sensuality,
    The berial of all beauty
        And portraiture preclair.   100
    Enter SOLACE, *the third Courtier, running.*
PLACEBO: By God, I see him at the last,
    As he were chasit, rinnand richt fast;
    He glowrs, even as he were agast,
        Or fleyit of a gaist.
    SOLACE, *drunk, at first addresses the audience.*
SOLACE: Wow! Wha saw ever sic a thrang!
    Methocht some said I had gane wrang.
    Had I help, I wald sing a sang
    With a richt merry noise!
    I have sic pleasure at my heart
    That gars me sing the treble part.   110
    Wald some good fellow fill the quart,
        That would my heart rejoice!
    Howbeit my coat be short and nippit,
    Thanks be to God I am weill hippit,
    Thocht all my gold may soon be grippit
        Into a penny purse.
    Thocht I a servant lang has been,
    My purchase is nocht worth a preen.
    I may sing Peebles On The Green
        For ocht that I may turse.   120
    What is my name? Can ye nocht guess?
    Sirs, ken ye nocht Sandy Solace?
    They callit my mother Bonny Bess,

124	*between the Bows*. A sexual *double entendre;* the 'Bows' were the burgh gateways.
125	*swyve*, copulate.
128	*mows*, joke
129	*speir*, ask.
131	*play-fere*, play-fellow.
136	*ring*, reign.
139	*fery-fary*, confusion.
144	*advance*, praise.
157	*what rack* (*of*), what matters.

That dwellt between the Bows.
Of twelve year auld she learned to swyve;
Thankit be the great god alive,
She made me fathers four or five –
   But doubt, this is na mows!
And if I lie, sirs, ye may speir.
But saw ye nocht the King come here? 130
I am a sporter and play-fere
   To that young King.
He said he wald, within short space,
To pass his time come to this place –
I pray to God to give him grace
   And lang to ring!
KING: My servant Solace, what gart ye tarry?
SOLACE *suddenly sees him.*
SOLACE: I wot not, sir, by sweet Sant Mary;
I have been in a fery-fary
   Or else into a trance! 140
Sir, I have seen, I you assure,
The fairest earthly crëature
That ever was formit by nature
   And maist for to advance.
To look on her is great delight,
With lippis reid and cheikis white.
I wald renunce all this warld quite
   To stand into her grace!
She is wanton and she is wise,
And cled she is in the new guise – 150
It would gar all your flesh uprise
   To look upon her face!
Were I a king, it suld be kend,
I sould not spare on her to spend
And this same nicht for her to send
   For my pleasure!
What rack of your prosperitie,
If ye want Sensuality!

169   *till*, to.

171   *Tanquam tabula rasa*, 'as it were a tablet clear of writing', hence 'Ready for good and ill'.

179–80   *a young . . . deil*, they will virtuously help him to sow his wild oats when he is young, since everyone knows 'there's na deil like an auld deil'.
180   *syne*, then, afterwards.

184   *whilk*, which; *lemand*, shining.

187   *Chastity*, the personage who appears later in the play.

I wald nocht give a silly flie
    For your treasure! 160
KING: Forsooth, my friends, I think ye are not wise,
  To counsel me to break commandëment
  Direckit by the Prince of Paradise;
  Considering ye knaw that mine intent
  Is for to be to God obedient,
  Wha does forbid men to be lecherous.
  Do I nocht sa, perchance I sall repent.
  Therefore I think your counsel odious
    The whilk ye gave me till,
  Because I have been to this day 170
  Tanquam tabula rasa,
    Ready for good and ill.
PLACEBO: Believe ye that we will beguile you,
  Or from your vertue we will wile you,
  Or with evil counsel for to file you?
    Baith into good and evil
  To tak your grace's part we grant,
  In all your deeds participant,
  Sa that ye be nocht a young sant
    And syne an auld deil. 180
WANTONNESS: Believe ye, sir, that lechery be sin?
  Na, trow nocht that! This is my reason why:
  First at the Roman Court will ye begin,
  Whilk is the lemand lamp of lechery,
  Where cardinals and bishops generally
  To luve ladies they think a pleasant sport,
  And out of Rome has banist Chastity,
  Wha with our prelates can get na resort.
SOLACE: Sir, while ye get a prudent queen,
  I think your Majesty serene 190
  Sould have a lusty concubene
    To play you withall:
  For I ken, by your quality,
  Ye want the gift of chastity.

29

195 *in nomine Domini*, 'in God's name'. The play's free use of
religious oaths reflects common speech but is also meant to
illustrate current superstition and ignorance, and here makes
a comment on Wantonness's counsel.

207 *the monks of Balmerino*. This monastery was in east Fife. The
reason for the special reference is not known.

213 *Kaity*, mistress.
214 *bummilbaty*, fool.
215 *Omnia probate*, 'prove all things', Saint Paul's injunction
(1 *Thessalonians*, v. 21) misapplied.

217 *awauk*, awake.
217–37 Hamer, in his edition, describes Sensuality as 'the type of
court prostitute', but she does not specially belong to the
Court. She is 'the perfite pattern of plesance', as Placebo later
describes her, and along with Covetice embodies the practical
religion of the governing classes. The 'fiery sphere' is the sun
and a reference is intended to the conventional May morning
of courtly love poetry.
218 *the natural dochter of Venus*, the true-born daughter of Venus.
In Scots Law 'natural' meant 'legitimate'.
222 *mak to Venus observance*, 'perform the rites of love', a phrase
common in Chaucer.
223 *chaumer*, chamber

Fall to, *in nomine Domini!*
 For this is my counsel!
I speak, sir, under protestatioun
That nane at me have indignatioun,
For all the prelates of this natioun,
 For the maist part   200
They think na shame to have a hure,
And some has three under their cure –
This to be true I'll you assure
 Ye sall wit efterwart.
Sir, knew ye all the matter through,
 To play ye wald begin.
Speir at the monks of Balmerino
 If lechery be sin!
PLACEBO: Sir, send furth Sandy Solace
 Or else your minion Wantonness,   210
And pray my Lady Prioress
 The sooth to declare,
If it be sin to tak a Kaity,
Or to live like a Bummilbaty.
The book says '*Omnia probate*',
 And nocht for to spare!
Music. LADY SENSUALITY *enters with her attendants,* HAMELI-
NESS, DANGER, FUND-JONET. *They take up their position at
the end of the stage remote from the* KING *and his courtiers, who do
not see them.*
SENSUALITY: Luvers awauk! Behauld the fiery sphere,
Behauld the natural dochter of Venus!
Behauld, luvers, this lusty lady clear,
The fresh fountain of knichtis amorous,   220
Replete with joys, dulce and delicious.
Or wha wald mak to Venus observance
In my mirthful chaumer melodious,

226   *hals*, neck.

235   *towart*, kindly.

243   *Danger*. In the allegory of the *Roman de la Rose* Danger,
       signifying prudent coyness or 'standoffishness', obstructed
       the lover in his pursuit of the Rose. Lindsay's Danger, asking
       for the support of Fund-Jonet, only affects coyness; her
       sister, Hameliness (Familiarity) does not trouble to affect it.
245   *Fund-Jonet*, literally, 'Foundling-Jonet'. Hamer, mis-deriving
       'Jonet' from 'gennet', a Spanish horse, describes her as 'a
       male assistant'. She is the Vekke, or go-between, of the
       Roman de la Rose, now frankly appearing as a bawd. She has
       taught Danger and Hameliness their business and has the
       conventional hoarse voice of the profession. Her girls would
       often be foundlings. Jonet is one of the most common of
       names among Scotswomen of that time and means 'mari-
       gold', cp. *The Kingis Quair*, st. 47, 'like to the floure-jonettis'.
248   *hass*, hoarse.

257   *japing*, copulating.

32

There sall they find all pastime and pleasance.
Behauld my heid, behauld my gay attire,
Behauld my hals, luvesome and lily-white;
Behauld my visage flammand as the fire,
Behauld my paps, of portrature perfite!
To look on me luvers has great delight;
Richt sa has all the kings of Christendom –   230
To them I have done pleasures infinite
And specially unto the Court of Rome.
Ae kiss of me were worth in a morning,
A million of gold to knicht or king.
And yet I am of nature sa towart
I let na luver pass with a sair heart.
Of my name, wald ye wit the verity,
Forsooth they call me Sensuality.
I hauld it best now, or we farther gang,
To Dame Venus let us go sing a sang   240
HAMELINESS: Madame, but tarrying
    We sall fall to and sing.
    Sister Danger, come near!
DANGER: Sister, sing this sang I may not
    Without the help of good Fund-Jonet.
    Fund-Jonet, ho! Come tak a part!
FUND-JONET: That sall I do with all my heart!
    Sister, howbeit that I am hass,
    I am content to beir a bass.
    Ye twa sould love me as your life –   250
    Ye knaw I learned you baith to swyve
    In my chaumer, ye wot weill where.
    Sensyne the fiend a man ye spare!
HAMELINESS: Fund-Jonet, fie, ye are to blame!
    To speak foul words, think ye na shame?
FUND-JONET: There is a hunder here sittand by
    That loves japing as weill as I,
    Micht they get it in privity.
    But wha begins the sang, let see!

260   *daws*, dawns.

260   The song is supplied here by verses of Alexander Montgomerie (c. 1550–c. 1598), the most prominent Scots poet at the close of the sixteenth century. His song is for May, the traditional season of love, and was appropriately introduced in the Edinburgh Festival production, Lindsay's song not having been preserved.

262   *shroudes*, put on their (green) clothing; *shaws*, woods.

264   *thrissel-cock*, male thrush.

266   *skailes*, clear.

269   *gowans*, daisies.

270   *lowe*, fire.

271   **roan**, rowan

278   *hiech*, high; *turses*, carry; *tynds*, horns.

280   *hurcheons*, hedge-hogs.

289   *maiks*, loves.

34

Hey, now the day daws,
The jolly cock craws,
Now shroudes the shaws
    Through Nature anon.
The thrissel-cock cries
On lovers that lies,
Now skailes the skies,
    The nicht is near gone.

The fieldis owerflows
With gowans that grows,
Where lilies like lowe is,
    As reid as the roan;
The turtle that true is,
With notes that renews,
Her party pursues,
    The nicht is near gone.

Now hartis with hinds,
Conform to their kinds,
Hiech turses their tynds
    On ground where they groan,
Now hurcheons, with hares,
Aye passes in pairs,
Whilk duly declares
    The nicht is near gone.

The season excels
Through sweetness that smells;
Now Cupid compels
    Our heartis each one,
On Venus wha wakes,
To muse on our maiks,
Then sing for their sakes
    The nicht is near gone.

304   *lyre*, face.

308-15 M.
310   *lair*, lore.

312   *cokks*, God's.

325   *tithands*, tidings.

During the singing of the song the KING *and his court see* SEN-
SUALITY *and her party.*

KING: Up, Wantonness, thou sleeps too lang!
    Methocht I heard a merry sang.
    I thee command in haste to gang
      See what yon mirth may mean.
WANTONNESS: I trow, sir, by the Trinity,
    Yon same is Sensuality,
    If it be she, soon sall I see
      That sovereign serene!
PLACEBO: Sir, she is mekill to advance,   300
    For she can baith play and dance,
    That perfite pattern of pleasance,
      A pearl of pulchritude!
    Saft as the silk is her white lyre,
    Her hair is like the golden wire,
    My heart burns in a flame of fire!
      I sweir you by the Rood,
    I think that free sa wonder fair,
    I wot weill she has na compair!
    War ye weill lernit at luve's lair,   310
      And syne had her seen,
    I wot, by cokks passioun,
    Ye wald mak supplicatioun,
    And spend on her a millioun,
      Her luve to obtene.
SOLACE: What say ye, sir? Are ye content
    That she come here incontinent?
    What vails your kingdom and your rent
      And all your great treasure,
    Without ye have a merry life,   320
    And cast aside all sturt and strife?
    And sa lang as ye want a wife,
      Sir, tak your pleasure!
KING: Forsooth, I wot not how it stands,
    But since I heard of your tithands

347   *deid*, death.

349   *fary*, busy.

351   M.

355   M. *back or edge*, decided one way or the other, perhaps referring to the 'flat or edge' of a sword.

My body trimmles, feet and hands,
　　And whiles is het as fire!
I trow Cupido with his dart
Has woundit me out-through the heart;
My spreit will fra my body part, 330
　　Get I nocht my desire!
Pass on, away, with diligence,
And bring her here to my presence!
Spare nocht for travel nor expense,
　　I care nocht for na cost!
Pass on your way soon, Wantonness,
And tak with you Sandy Solace,
And bring that Lady to this place,
　　Or else I am but lost!
Commend me to that sweetest thing, 340
Present her with this same rich ring,
And say I lie in languishing,
　　Except she mak remede!
With siching sair I am but shent
Without she come incontinent,
My heavy langour to relent
　　And save me now fra deid!
WANTONNESS: Doubt ye nocht, sir, but we will get her.
　　We shall be fary for to fet her.
　　But, faith, we wald speed all the better, 350
　　　Had we a bag for wage!
SOLACE: Sir! Let na sorrow in you sink,
　　But give us ducats for to drink,
　　And we sall never sleep a wink
　　　Till it be back or edge.
　　The KING *gives them a purse.*
KING: I pray you, speed you soon again!
WANTONNESS: Yea, of this sang, sir, we are fain!
　　We sall neither spare for wind nor rain
　　　Till our day's wark be done!
　　Fareweill, for we are at the flicht! 360

378   *forfare*, die.

380   *mou*, mouth.

383   *mak collatioun*, dine.

385   *fra-hand*, forthwith.

390   *band*, vow.

Placebo, rule our Roy at richt.
We sall be here, man, or midnicht
 Thocht we march with the moon!
A gay march. SOLACE *and* WANTONNESS *make a detour of the*
stage and come to SENSUALITY *and her court.*
Pastime with pleasance and great prosperity
Be to you, Sovereign Sensuality!
SENSUALITY: Sirs, ye are welcome. Where go ye? East or West?
WANTONNESS: In faith, I trow we be at the farrest!
SENSUALITY: What is your name? I pray you sir, declare!
WANTONNESS: Marry, Wantonness, the King's secretair.
SENSUALITY: What king is that, whilk has so gay a boy? 370
WANTONNESS: Humanity, that richt redoubtit Roy,
 Wha does commend him to you heartfully,
 And sends you here a ring with a ruby,
 In taken that above all crëature
 He has chosen you to be his Paramour:
 He bade me say that he will be but deid,
 Without that ye mak hastily remede.
SENSUALITY: How can I help him, althocht he sould forfare?
 Ye ken richt weill I am na Medciner.
SOLACE: A kiss of your sweet mou, in a morning,   380
 To his sickness micht be great comforting.
 And als he maks you supplicatioun
 This nicht to mak with him collatioun.
SENSUALITY: I thank his grace of his benevolence!
 Good sirs, I sall be ready even fra-hand.
 In me there sall be fund na negligence,
 Baith nicht and day, when his grace will demand.
 Pass ye before, and say I am cumand
 And thinks richt lang to have of him a sicht.
 And I to Venus mak a faithful band,   390
 That in his arms I think to lie all nicht.
WANTONNESS: That sall be done . . . but yet or I hame pass,
 Here I protest for Hameliness, your lass.
SENSUALITY: She sall be at command, sir, when ye will:

397   *gamond*, a lively capering dance.

401   *tyst*, entice.

402–3   *The fiend ... marriage*, 'the devil a penny of dowry he will get by this marriage!'

405   *brank*, prance.

406   *wreistit*, wrested.

410   *speir*, ask.

415   *Him ... hell.* According to a medieval legend, deriving from the apocryphal gospel of *Nicodemus*, during the days of his burial Christ descended into hell and plundered ('herriet'), i.e. rescued, the souls of the faithful.

422   *perqueir*, by heart.

423   *gin*, tricks.

426   *clap*, fondle.

I traist she sall find you flinging your fill!

WANTONNESS: Now hey for joy and mirth I dance!

Music, which accompanies the speech.

Tak there a gay gamond of France!

Am I nocht worthy to advance

    That am sa good a page,

And that sa speedily can rin   400

To tyst my maister unto sin?

The fiend a penny he will win

    Of this his marriage!

A dance, during which WANTONNESS *and* PLACEBO *skip back to the* KING. *On the way* WANTONNESS *pretends to hurt his leg.*

(to audience): I think this day to win great thank!

Hey, as a bridlit cat I brank!

Alas, I have wreistit my shank . . .

    Yet I gang, by Sant Michael!

Whilk of my legs, sirs, as ye trow,

Was it that I did hurt even now?

But whereto sould I speir at you –   410

    I think they baith are hale!

He turns to the KING. *The music ends.*

Good morrow, Maister, by the Mess!

KING: Welcome, my minion Wantonness!

How has thou sped in thy travail?

WANTONNESS: Richt weill, by Him that herriet hell!

Your errand is weil done!

KING *(transported)*: Then, Wantonness, full weill is me!

Thou hast deservit baith meat and fee,

    By Him that made the moon!

(Anxiously) There is ae thing that I wald speir . . .   420

What sall I do when she comes here?

For I knaw nocht the craft perqueir

    Of lovers, gin;

Therefore at length ye mon me leir

    How to begin.

WANTONNESS: To kiss her and clap her, sir, be not affeared!

429   *tail*, the train or very long skirt then fashionable; *tent weill*, take good care of.

433   *preive*, try.

440   *visie*, visit.

443-9   M.

448   *the cures*, the charge.

455   *lustiness*, pleasure.

She will not shrink, thocht ye kiss her, a span within the beard.
If ye think, that she thinks shame, then hide the bairnis een
With her tail, and tent her weill, ye wot what I mean!
Will ye give me leave, sir, first to go to,   430
And I sall learn you the cues, how ye sall do?
KING: God forbid, Wantonness, that I give you leave!
Thou art ower perilous a page sic practiks to preive!
WANTONNESS *sees* SENSUALITY.
Wantonness: Now, sir, preive as ye please, I see her cumand!
Order you with gravity, and we sall by you stand.

Music. The KING *and his courtiers prepare to welcome* SEN-
SUALITY. *She apart first makes her vow to Venus, accompanied by
music.*

SENSUALITY: O Venus goddess, unto thy celsitude
I give laud, gloir, honour and reverence,
Whilk grantit me sic perfite pulchritude.
I mak a vow, with humill observance,
Richt reverently thy temple to visie   440
With sacrifice unto thy deitie!
To every state I am sa agreabill
That few or nane refuses me at all –
Papes, patriarchs, nor prelates venerabill,
Common people, nor princes temporal,
But subject all to me Dame Sensual!
Sa sall it be ay while the warld endures,
And specially where youthage has the cures.

She turns towards the KING.

And now my way I mon advance
Unto a prince of great puissance,   450
Whom young men has in governance,
    Rolland into his rage.
I am richt glad, I you assure,
That potent prince to get in cure,
Wha is of lustiness the lure
    And greatest of courage.

45

458   *celsitude*, Highness.

462   *lammer*, amber, or rather ambergris, a grey, wax-like sub-
       stance prized for its perfume.

467   *ye's*, you will.

470   *play cap-out*, empty the 'cap' or drinking-bowl.
471   *len*, lend; *that batty tout*. In the 1552 version 'thy batty towt',
       in the 1554 one 'that batye tout'. Editors have made no sense
       of this, but 'batty' means plump, well-bodied, and 'tout'
       means 'drink', hence 'that lusty drink'.
474   *gotten upon the gumes*, have made love.

476   *lumes*, instruments.

484   *fling*, dance.

The music ends. A detour brings her at last to the KING.
O potent prince, of pulchritude preclair,
God Cupido preserve your celsitude!
And Dame Venus mot keep your corse from care,
As I wald she sould keep my awn heart blude!   460
KING: Welcome to me, peerless of pulchritude!
  Welcome to me, thou sweeter nor the lammer,
  Whilk has me made of all dolour denude!
  Solace, convoy this lady to my chaumer.
SENSUALITY: I gae this gait with richt good will.
  Sir Wantonness, tarry ye still;
  And Hameliness, the cup ye's fill
    And beir him company!
Music, which continues till the departure of KING *and party.*
HAMELINESS: That sall I do withouten doubt,
  For he and I sall play cap-out!   470
WANTONNESS: Now lady, len me that batty tout.
    Fill in, for I am dry.
  Your dame, by this, truly,
  Has gotten upon the gumes!
  What rack thocht ye and I
  Go join our jousting lumes?
HAMELINESS: Content I am with richt good will,
  Whenever ye are ready,
  All your pleasure to fulfill.
WANTONNESS: Now weill said, by our Lady!   480
  I'll beir my maister company,
    As lang as I endure!
  If he be whiskand wantonly,
    We sall fling on the flure!
The KING *and his party go into the arbour at the top of the stage.*
As they disappear GOOD COUNSEL, *a bearded figure, hobbles in*
and addresses the audience.
GOOD COUNSEL: Consider, my sovereigns, I you beseek,
  The cause maist principal of my coming.
  Princes nor potestates are nocht worth a leek,

505-6   *our guiders . . . day.* James III was killed in the rebellion of 1488, James IV at the battle of Flodden, 1513, and James V died after the rout of Solway Moss, 1542.

507   *lichtlyt,* scorned.

522   *traist,* trust; *stylet,* honoured.

Be they not guidit by my good governing.
There was never emperor, conqueror nor king,
Without my wisdom that micht their weal advance.   490
My name is Good Counsel, without feignyeing.
Lords for lack of my law are brocht to mischance,
And so, for conclusioun,
Wha guides them nocht by Good Counsel,
All in vain is their travail,
And finally fortune sall them fail,
And bring them to confusioun.
    And this I understand,
For I have made my residence
With hie princes of great puissance,   500
In England, Italy and France,
    And mony other land.
But out of Scotland, wae alace,
I have been banissit lang space –
That gars our guiders all want grace,
And die before their day!
Because they lichtlyt Good Counsel,
Fortune turnit on them her sail,
Whilk brocht this realm to meikle bale –
    Wha can the contrair say?   510
My lords, I came nocht here to lie;
Waes me for King Humanity,
Owrrset with Sensuality
    In th'entrie of his ring,
Through vicious counsel insolent!
Sa they may get riches or rent,
To his weilfare they tak na tent,
    Nor what sall be the ending!
For wald the King be guidit yet with reason
And on mis-doers mak punitioun,   520
Howbeit that I lang time has been exilet
I traist in God my name sall yet be stylet.
Sa till I see God send mair of his grace,

49   D

525   FLATTERY. The chief Vice in the play enters in many-coloured dress with a fool's patter. His Scots audience has known him as the Abbot of Unreason – in England the Lord of Misrule – of the Christmas-tide revels, but all Christendom knows him. Only a true fool, he says, would risk his life at sea – the satiric convention of the ship of fools seems to be invoked here – but he went to get himself a 'new array', and the audience will now see their 'awn fool' foster folly everywhere once again.

527   *begariet*, adorned.

532   *stormsted*, storm-stayed; *sen*, since; *Yule*, Christmas.

540   *Hail*, Haul.

541   *a-luff*, steer close to the wind.

542   *raipes*, ropes; *fleid*, frightened.

543   *Roy*, King. Flattery compares himself to the King of the Bean, the person chosen, by the picking of a bean from a cake, to be master of the revels on Twelfth Day (6th January).

545   *waws*, waves.

550   *yeid*, went.

553   *feill*, know.

554   *cast*, ploy.

555   FALSET. Generally signifies falsehood, but particularly false report, misrepresentation. See his accusation of Verity and his hanging speech at the close of the play.

556   *sair*, harm

I purpose to repose me in this place.

GOOD COUNSEL *draws apart.* FLATTERY, *the first of the Three Vices to appear, rushes in, dressed in motley.*

FLATTERY: Mak room, sirs, ho! that I may rin!

Lo, see how I am new come in,
   Begariet all with sindry hues!
Let be your din till I begin,
   And I sall shaw you of my news!
Throuchout all Christendom I have passed   530
And am come here now at the last,
Stormsted by sea ay sen Yule Day,
That we were fain to hew our mast,
Nocht half a mile beyond the May.
But now amang you I will remain,
I purpose never to sail again,
   To put my life in chance of watter!
Was never seen sic wind and rain,
   Nor of shipmen sic clitter-clatter.
Some bade 'Hail!', some bade 'Stand-by!'   540
'On starboard ho!' 'A-luff, fie, fie!'
   While all the raipes began to rattle.
Was never Roy sa fleid as I,
   When all the sails played brittle-brattle!
To see the waws, it was a wonder,
And wind, that rave the sails in sunder!
Now am I scapet fra that affray;
What say ye, sirs, am I nocht gay?
   See ye nocht Flattery, your awn fool,
That yeid to mak this new array?   550
   Was I nocht here with you at Yule?
Yes, by my faith, I think on weill!
Where are my fellows, that wald I feill?
   We sould have come here for a cast!
Ho, Falset, ho!

FALSET *enters.*

FALSET: Wae sair the Deil!

562 *limmer*, rascal; *loon*, knave.

566 *thae*, these.

573 *felon*, great; *fray*, fear.

578 *That . . . mare*, 'Your purpose is the same as mine' (*samin*, same).
579 *sen*, since.

587 *steir him*, take action

590 *confusion*, ruin

    Wha's that that cries for me sa fast?
FLATTERY: Why, Falset, brother, knawis thou not me?
    I am thy brother, Flattery!
FALSET: Now let me brace thee in my arms!
    When freindis meetis, heartis warms!   560
    They embrace.
FLATTERY: Where is Deceit, that limmer loon?
FALSET: I left him drinkand in the toun.
    He will be here incontinent.
FLATTERY: Now by the Haily Sacrament,
    Thae tidings comforts all my heart!
    He is richt crafty as ye ken,
    And counsellor to the Merchant-men!
    Enter DECEIT.
DECEIT: *Bon jour*, brother, with all my heart,
    Here am I come to tak your part   570
        Baith into good and evil!
    I met Good Counsel by the way,
    Wha pat me in a felon fray –
        I give him to the Deil!
    How came ye here, I pray you tell me.
FALSET: Marry, to seek King Humanity!
DECEIT: Now, by the good lady that me bare,
    That samin horse in my awn mare!
    Sen we three seeks yon noble King,
    Let us devise some subtle thing!   580
    Also I pray you as your brother,
    That we, ilk ane, be true to other.
    I pray to God, nor I be hangit,
    But I sall die or ye be wrangit!
FALSET: What is thy counsel that we do?
DECEIT: Marry, sirs, this is my counsel, lo!
    Fra time the King begin to steir him,
    Marry! Good Counsel I dread come near him,
    And be we knawin with Correctioun,
    It will be our confusioun.   590

596   *clerkis claithing.* Flattery disguises himself as a friar, Falsehood
        as a Doctor in his gown and hood, Deceit as a priest, in which
        capacity he performs the mock baptisms.
598   *new come out of France,* learned men lately returned from studies
        in France.

614   'What does it matter if I can flatter and cajole?'

619–25 M.

Therefore, my dear brether, devise
To find some toy of the new guise.
FLATTERY: Marry, I shall find a thousand wiles.
We mon turn our claiths, and change our styles
And disaguise us, that na man ken us.
Has na man clerkis claithing to len us?
And let us keep grave countenance,
As we were new come out of France!
DECEIT: Now, by my saul, that is weill deviset!
Ye sall see me soon disaguiset.   600
FALSET: And sa sall I, man, by the Rood!
Now, some good fellow, len me a hood!
The THREE VICES *disguise themselves in clothes from a   bundle*
which DECEIT *has brought on.*
DECEIT: Now am I buskit, and wha can spy?
The Deil stick me, if this be I!
If this be I, or nocht, I cannot weil say,
Or has the Fiend or Fairy-folk borne me away?
FALSET: What says thou of my gay garmoun?
DECEIT: I say thou looks even like a loon.
Now, brother Flattery, what do ye?
What kind of man shape ye to be?   610
FLATTERY: Now, by my faith, my brother dear,
I will ga counterfeit a freir!
DECEIT: A freir? Whereto? Ye cannot preach.
FLATTERY: What rack but I can flatter and fleech?
Perchance I'll come to that honour,
To be the Kingis confessour!
Poor freirs are free at any feast
And marshallt ay amang the best!
Good wives will nevir let freiris want.
For why, they are their confessours,   620
Their prudent heavenly counselours.
Therefore wives plainly taks their parts
And shaws the secrets of their hearts
To freirs, with better will I trow

627   *a cowl of Tullilum.* There was a Carmelite monastery at this place, on the west side of Perth.

628   *porteous,* breviary.

639   *godbairn,* baptismal.

644   *ance,* once.

650   *lurdan,* lazy.

656   *crack and clatter,* lie and chatter.

Nor they do to their bedfellow!
DECEIT has fetched a monk's cowl.
DECEIT: Here is thy gaining, all and some.
  That is a cowl of Tullilum!
FLATTERY: Wha has a porteous to len me?
  The fiend a saul, I trow, will ken me!
  The BISHOP tosses down a breviary.
FALSET: We mon do mair yet, by Sant James!   630
  For we mon all three change our names.
  Christen me and I sall baptise thee.
  There follows a mock ceremony.
DECEIT: By God and thereabout may it be!
  How will thou call me, I pray thee tell!
FALSET: I wot not how to call mysell!
DECEIT: But yet ance name the bairnis name!
FALSET: Discretioun, Discretioun in God's name!
DECEIT: I need not now to care for thrift,
  But what sall be my Godbairn gift?
FALSET: I give you all the deils of hell!   640
DECEIT: Na, brother, hauld that to yoursell!
  Now, sit doun! Let me baptise thee!
  I wot not what they name sould be.
FALSET: But yet ance name the bairnis name!
DECEIT: Sapience, Sapience, in God's name!
FLATTERY: Brother, Deceit, come baptise me!
DECEIT: Then sit doun lawly on thy knee!
FLATTERY: Now, brother, name the bairnis name.
DECEIT: Devotioun in the devil's name!
  He splashes FLATTERY with water.
FLATTERY: The deil resaive thee, lurdan loon!   650
  Thou has wet all my new shaven croun!
DECEIT: Devotioun, Sapience, and Discretioun –
  We three may rule this regioun.
  We sall find mony crafty things
  For to beguile a hunder kings!
  For thou can richt weill crack and clatter,

57

667   *learand*, learning.

676   *bent*, field.

686   *the clippit croun*, the friar's tonsure.

And I sall feignye and (*to* FLATTERY) thou sall flatter.

FLATTERY: But I wald have, or we departit,
　A drink to mak us better heartit.

DECEIT: Weil said, by Him that herriet hell,　　　　　660
　I was even thinkand that mysell!
　While the THREE VICES *are drinking, the* KING *appears leading*
　SENSUALITY *from the arbour.*

KING: Now where is Placebo and Solace?
　Where is my minion Wantonness?
　Wantonness, ho! Come to me soon!
　WANTONNESS *and* HAMELINESS *appear.*

WANTONNESS: Why cried ye, sir, till I had done?

KING: What was thou doand, tell me that?

WANTONNESS: Marry, learand how my father me gat!
　I wot not how it stands, but doubt
　Methinks the warld rins round about!

KING: And sa think I, man, by my thrift!　　　　　670
　I see fifteen moons in the lift.
　SOLACE, PLACEBO *and* DANGER *appear.*

SOLACE: Now shaw me, sir, I you exhort,
　How are ye of your love content?
　Think ye not this a merry sport?

KING: Yea, that I do in verament!
　The KING *spies the* THREE VICES.
　What bairns are yon upon the bent?
　I did not see them all this day.

WANTONNESS: They will be here incontinent.
　Stand still and hear what they will say.
　The THREE VICES *come forward and salute the* KING.

VICES: Laud, honour, gloir, triumph and victory,　　　　680
　Be to your maist excellent Majesty!

KING: Ye are welcome, good friends, by the Rood!
　Appearandly ye seem some men of good.
　What are your names, tell me without delay.

DECEIT: Discretioun, sir, is my name perfay.

KING: What is your name, sir, with the clippit croun?

59

688   *Sant Jame.* The brother of John the Evangelist, his body was said to be at Compostella in Spain.

695–699   *they call me Thin-Drink.* Lindsay's pun on 'Sapience' does not seem to have been noted. To Falsehood 'Sapience' sounds the same as 'Sypiens' or 'Sypins', the oozings or dregs of a cask.
697   *plat,* blow.

708–9   M.
703   *heich,* high.

717   *thesaurar,* treasurer.

720   *Sant Ann,* the mother of the Virgin Mary.

FLATTERY: But doubt my name is callit Devotioun.
KING: Welcome, Devotioun, by Sant Jame!
   Now, sirrah, tell what is your name?
FALSET: Marry, sir, they call me . . what call they me?   690
   (*Aside*) I wot not well, but if I lie!
KING: Can thou nocht tell what is thy name?
FALSET: I kend it when I cam fra hame!
KING: What ails thou cannot shaw it now?
FALSET (*confused*): Marry, they call me Thin-Drink, I trow.
KING: Thin-Drink, what kind of name is that?
DECEIT: Sapience, thou serves to bear a plat!
   Methinks thou shaws thee not weil-wittit.
FALSET: Sypiens, sir, Sypiens, marry, now ye hit it!
   FLATTERY *brushes* FALSET *aside.*
FLATTERY: Sir, if ye please to let me say,   700
   That same is Sapientia!
FALSET: That same is it, by Sant Michael!
KING: Why could thou not tell it thysell?
FALSET: I pray your grace to pardon me.
   And I sall shaw the verity –
   I am sa full of Sapience
   That sometime I will tak a trance.
   My spreit was reft fra my body,
   Now heich aboon the Trinity.
KING: Sapience sould be a man of good.   710
FALSET: Sir, ye may knaw that by my hood!
KING: Now have I Sapience and Discretioun,
   How can I fail to rule this regioun?
   And Devotioun to be my Confessour!
   Thir three came in a happy hour.
   to FALSEHOOD) Here I mak thee my secretar!
   (*to* DECEIT) And thou sall be my thesaurar!
   (*to* FLATTERY) And thou sall be my counsellour
   In spritual things, and confessour.
FLATTERY: I sweir to you, sir, by Sant Ann,   720
   Ye met never with a wiser man,

724   *feill*, knowledge.

726   *astronomy*. Astrology seems to be indicated by the collocation
        with the pseudo-sciences of alchemy, physiognomy,
        palmestry.

729   *quelling of the quintessence*, extracting the fifth essence, the sub-
        stance of which the heavily bodies were imagined to consist,
        in order to transmute metals into gold.

732   *To mak multiplicatioun*, to transmute into gold.

735   *loons*, rascals.

737–43 The comic juxtaposition of foreign conquests and Scots
        place-names parodies the list of King Arthur's conquests as
        given in romance and chronicle. See the alliterative *Morte
        Arthur* (ll. 26–47) and Andrew Wyntoun's chronicle (ed.
        Amours, Scottish Text Society, vol. 4, p. 19). 'Danskin' is
        Danzig; 'Almane' is Germany; 'Spitalfield' is probably the
        village of this name in Perthshire; 'Ruglen' is Rutherglen
        beside Glasgow; Corstorphine was then a village on the west
        side of Edinburgh.

745   *A-per-se*, an incomparable person, like one of the Nine Nobles
        or Worthies (first celebrated in *The Roman d'Alexandre*), of
        whom the three Christian ones were Arthur, Charlemagne,
        Godfrey of Boulogne.

748   *loof*, palm.

755   *sa white a face*, considered a sign of noble lineage.

For mony a craft, sir, do I can,
   Were they weill knawn.
I have na feill of flattery,
But fosterit with philosophy,
A strang man in astronomy,
Whilk sall be soon shawn!

FALSET: And I have great intelligence
  In quelling of the quintessence,
  But to preive my experience,   730
    Sir, len me forty crouns
  To mak multiplicatioun;
  And tak my obligatioun,
  If we mak false narratioun,
    Hald us for very loons!

DECEIT: Sir, I ken by your physnomy,
  Ye sall conqueis, or else I lie,
  Danskin, Denmark and all Almane,
  Spitalfield and the Realm of Spain.
  Ye sall have at your governance   740
  Renfrew, and the Realm of France,
  Yea, Ruglen and the Toun of Rome,
  Corstorphine and all Christendom.
  Whereto, sir, by the Trinity
  Ye are a very A-per-se!

FLATTERY: Sir, when I dwelt in Italy,
  I leirit the craft of palmistry.
  Shaw me the loof, sir, of your hand,
  And I sall mak you understand
  If your grace be infortunate   750
  Or if ye be predestinate.
  The KING shows his hand.
  I see ye will have fifteen queens
  And fifteen score of concubenes!
  The Virgin Mary save your grace,
  Saw ever man sa white a face,
  Sa great an arm, sa fair a hand!

759   *dang*, struck.

767   *carl*, rogue.

777   *lyart*, grey.

785   *swith*, quick; *unsel*, wretch.

789   *devoid*, leave.

There's nocht sic a leg in all this land!
Were ye in arms, I think na wonder,
Howbeit ye dang doun fifteen hunder.
KING: Ye are richt welcome, by the Rood,   760
   Ye seem to be three men of good.
   GOOD COUNSEL *takes up a more prominent position.*
   But wha is yon that stands so still?
   Go spy and speir what is his will.
   And if he yearnis my presence,
   Bring him to me with diligence.
   The THREE VICES *quickly confer.*
FLATTERY: I dreid full sair by God himsel,
   That yon old carl be Good Counsel!
   Get he ance to the King's presence,
   We three will get na audience!
DECEIT: That matter I sall tak on hand,   770
   And say it is the King's command,
   That he anon devoid this place
   And come not near the Kingis grace,
   And that under the pain of treason!
FLATTERY: Brother, I hald your counsel reason.
   Now let us hear what he will say.
   He addresses GOOD COUNSEL.
   Auld lyart beard, good day, good day!
GOOD COUNSEL: Good day again, sirs, by the Rood.
   I pray God mak you men of good.
DECEIT: Pray not for us to Lord nor Lady,   780
   For we are men of good already!
   Sir, shaw to us what is your name.
GOOD COUNSEL: Good Counsel they call me at hame.
FALSET: What says thou, carl, are thou Good Counsel?
   Swith, pack thee hence, unhappy unsel!
GOOD COUNSEL: I pray you, sirs, give me licence,
   To come ance to the King's presence
   To speak but twa words to his grace.
FLATTERY: Swith, hureson carl, devoid this place!

65   E

791   *mak it teuch*, swagger.

804   *bousteous*, rough.

806   *laithly*, loathsome; *lurdan*, good-for-nothing.

809   *the Thievis Hole*, the stocks.

811   *pastance*, pleasure.

813   *hurley-hacket*, sledging.
814   *corses*, bodies.

GOOD COUNSEL: Brother, I ken you weill eneuch, 790
    Howbeit ye mak it never sa teuch –
    Flattery, Deceit and False-Report,
    That will not suffer to resort
    Good Counsel to the King's presence.
DECEIT: Swith, hureson carl, ga pack thee hence!
    If ever thou come this gait again,
    I vow to God thou sall be slain!
    They set upon GOOD COUNSEL *and push him from the stage.*
GOOD COUNSEL: Sen at this time I can get na presence,
    Is na remede but tak in patience.
    But when youth-heid has blawn his wanton blast, 800
    Then sall Good Counsel rule him at the last!
    GOOD COUNSEL *is chased out. The* THREE VICES *return to the*
    KING.
KING: What gart you bide sa lang fra my presence?
    I think it lang since ye departit thence.
    What man was yon, with a great bousteous beard?
    Methocht he made you all three very feared!
DECEIT: It was a laithly lurdan loon,
    Come to break booths into this toun!
    We have gart bind him with a pole
    And send him to the Thievis Hole.
KING: Let him sit there with a mischance! 810
    And let us go to our pastance!
WANTONNESS: Better go revel at the racket,
    Or else go to the hurley-hacket,
    Or then to shaw our courtly corses
    Ga see wha best can rin their horses.
    As they make to move SOLACE *stops them.*
SOLACE: Na, Sovereign, or we farther gang,
    Gar Sensuality sing a sang.

818   The excellent song by Alexander Scott (*floruit* c. 1540–70) used in the Edinburgh Festival production has been retained here, Lindsay's song not having been recorded. Scott is best known for his love poems.

820   *sa hie has set her*, has made her so disdainful.

823   *may*, maid.

825   *plet*, fold.

828   *glaikit*, stupid.

838   *Diligite . . . terram*, is translated by the following line and is from the apocryphal *Book of Wisdom*, l.1.

839–51   M.

(They sing.)

To luve unluvet it is a pain,
For she that is my sovereign
   Some wanton man sa hie has set her   820
That I can get na luve again,
   But breks my heart, and nocht the better!

When that I went with that sweet may,
To dance, to sing, to sport and play,
   And ofttimes in my armis plet her,
I do now murn baith nicht and day
   And breaks my heart, and nocht the better!

Whatten a glaikit fool am I,
To slay mysell with melancholy,
Sen weill I ken I may nocht get her!   830
Or what sould be the cause and why
   To brek my heart, and nocht the better!

My heart, sen thou may nocht her please,
Adieu! As good luve comes as gaes!
   Go choose another and forget her!
God give him dolour and disease
   That breks their heart, and nocht the better!

As the music ends, VERITY *enters, a Puritan maid holding a Bible.*
She stands apart, but FLATTERY *goes out to peer at her as she speaks.*
VERITY: *Diligite Justitiam qui judicatis terram.*
Love Justice, ye wha has a Judge's cure
In earth, and dreid the awful Judgëment   840
Of Him that sall come judge baith rich and poor
Richt terribly, with bluidy woundis rent.
That dreidfull day into your hearts imprent,
Believand weill how and what manner ye
Use justice here to others, there at length

69

860   *novells*, news.

862   *by books and bells*, more fully, 'with bell, book and candle'. In the form of excommunication a book is closed, a candle put out and a bell rung. Flattery fears that he and his fellows will be wholly excluded from the king's company.

866   *Sant Bride*, see note to 1.1527.

874   *beirand the New Testament*. Only English versions were available in print, the first authorised printing of a vernacular New Testament being at London in 1536.

875   M.

876–79   Kemp's text gives this speech to the Bishop.

That day but doubt sa sall ye judgit be.
And if ye wald your subjects were weill given,
Then vertuously begin the dance yoursell,
Going before, then they anon, I ween,
Sall follow you, either to heaven or hell.   850
If men of me wald have intelligence,
Or knaw my name, they call me Verity.
Of Christis law I have experience,
And has owrsailit mony stormy sea.
Now am I seekand King Humanity,
For of his grace I have good esperance.
Fra time that he acquaintit be with me,
His honour and heich gloir I sall advance.
    As FLATTERY *returns* DECEIT *greets him.*
DECEIT: Good day, Father, where have you been?
    Declare to us of your novells.   860
FLATTERY: There is now lichtit on the green,
    Dame Verity, by books and bells!
    But come she to the King's presence,
    There is na boot for us to bide!
    Therefore I rede us, all go hence!
FALSET: That will we nocht yet, by Sant Bride!
    But we sall either gang or ride
    To Lords of Sprituality,
    And gar them trow yon bag of pride
    Has spoken manifest heresy!   870
    Here the THREE VICES *go to the* SPIRITUAL ESTATE.
FLATTERY: O reverent fathers of the Sprutual State,
    We counsel you be wise and vigilant!
    Dame Verity has lichtit now of late,
    And in her hand beirand the New Testament!
    The SPIRITUAL ESTATE *confer in undertones for a moment.*
BISHOP: What is your counsel, brether, now let see.
ABBOT: I hauld it best that we incontinent
    Gar hauld her fast into captivity
    Unto the thrid day of the Parliament

880–3   M.

890   *dulce*, sweet.

894   *forfare*, suffer.

901–2   M.

And then accuse her of her heresy.

BISHOP: Sir Parson, ye sall be my commissair,   880
　　And ye, Sir Freir, because ye can declare
　　The haill process, pass with him in commissioun.
　　Pass all together with my braid benisoun!
　　The THREE VICES *approach* VERITY.

FLATTERY: What book is that, harlot, in thy hand?
　　He looks at it.
　　Out! Wallaway! This is the New Testament!
　　In Inglis tongue, and prentit in Ingland!
　　Heresy, heresy! Fire, fire, incontinent!

VERITY: Forsooth, my friend, ye have a wrang judgment,
　　For in this Book there is na heresy,
　　But our Christ's word, richt dulce and redolent,   890
　　A springing well of sincere verity!

DECEIT: Come on your way, for all your yellow locks!
　　Your wanton words but doubt ye sall repent!
　　This nicht ye sall forfare a pair of stocks,
　　And syne, the morn, be brocht to thole judgment.
　　VERITY *falls on her knees, not to the* VICES *but to Heaven.*

VERITY: Get up, thou sleepis all too lang, O Lord,
　　And mak some reasonable reformatioun
　　On them that does tramp doun Thy gracious Word,
　　And has a deidly indignatioun
　　At them wha maks maist true narratioun!   900
　　Now, lords, do as ye list.
　　I have na mair to say.

FLATTERY: Sit doun and tak you rest
　　All nicht till it be day!
　　They put VERITY *in the stocks, and return to* SPIRITUALITY.

DECEIT: My lord, we have with diligence,
　　Bucklet up weill yon blethran bard!

BISHOP: I think ye serve good recompense.
　　Tak thir ten crowns for your reward!
　　CHASTITY *enters intoning to herself a Latin Hymn.*

CHASTITY: How lang sall this inconstant warld endure?

912   *harbryless*, shelterless.

940   *uncouth shire*, strange land.

That I sould banist be sa lang, alas!   910
Few crëatures, or nane, taks of me cure,
Whilk gars me mony nicht lie harbryless!
DILIGENCE: Lady, I pray you shaw to me your name.
It does me noy, your lamentatioun!
CHASTITY: My freind, thereof I need nocht to think shame,
Dame Chastity, banist from toun to toun.
DILIGENCE: Then pass to ladies of religioun,
Whilk maks their vow to observe chastity.
Lo, where there sits a Prioress of renoun
Amang the rest of Sprituality.   920
DILIGENCE *points out the* PRIORESS, *who is one of the* SPIRITUAL
ESTATE.
CHASTITY: I grant yon lady has vowit chastity,
For her professioun thereto sould accord.
She made that vow for an abbessy,
But nocht for Christ Jesus our Lord.
I sall observe your counsel if I may.
Come on and hear what yon lady will say.
DILIGENCE *and* CHASTITY *approach the* PRIORESS.
My prudent, lusty Lady Prioress,
Remember how ye did vow chastity;
Madame, I pray you of your gentleness
That ye wald please to have of me pity   930
And this ae nicht to give me harboury!
PRIORESS: Pass hence, Madame, by Christ ye come nocht here!
Ye are contrair to my complexioun!
Gang seek ludging at some auld monk or freir,
Perchance they will be your protectioun.
Or to prelates mak your progressioun,
Whilk are obleist to you as weill as I!
Dame Sensual has given directioun
You to exclude out of my company!
CHASTITY *now addresses the* CHURCHMEN.
CHASTITY: Lords, I have past through mony uncouth shire, 940
But in this land I can get na ludging!

75

953   *the Queen of Fairy*, Hecate, the mistress of spirits, goblins, etc.

956   *traist*, trust.

959   *dortour*, dormitory; *dang*, beat.

975   *on steir*, astir. A *soutar* is a shoemaker.
976   *rin arear*, run off.

Of my name if ye wald have knawledging,
Forsooth, my lords, they call me Chastity.
I you beseek, of your graces bening,
Give me ludging this nicht for charity.
BISHOP: Pass on, Madame, we knaw you nocht!
Or by Him that the warld has wrocht,
Your coming sall be richt dear bocht,
 If ye mak langer tarry!
ABBOT: But doubt we will baith live and die   950
 With our love Sensuality.
We will have na mair deal with thee
 Then with the Queen of Fairy!
PARSON: Pass hame amang the Nuns and dwell,
 Whilk are of chastity the well.
I traist they will with book and bell
 Resaive you in their closter!
CHASTITY: Sir, when I was the Nuns amang,
Out of their dortour they me dang,
And wald nocht let me bide sa lang   960
 To say my Paternoster.
I see na grace there for to get.
I hald it best, or it be late,
For to go prove the temporal state
 If they will me resaive
CHASTITY *crosses to the* TEMPORAL ESTATE.
Good day, my lord Temporality,
And you, Merchant of gravity;
Full fain wald I have harboury,
 To ludge amang the lave.
LORD: Forsooth, we wald be weill content   970
To harbour you with good intent,
Were nocht we have impediment –
 For-why we twa are marriet!
MERCHANT: But wist our wives that ye were here,
They wald mak all this toun on steir,
Therefore we rede you, rin arear,

977   *miscarryt*, ill treated.
978   *ingine*, skill; *men of craft*, craftsmen, men belonging to the
          Crafts.
978   *S.D.* JENNIE does not appear in Kemp's version.
978–1034 As Hamer notes, Lindsay here exploits two comic traditions,
          the alleged want of virility in cobblers and tailors, which
          makes them peculiarly sympathetic to Chastity, and the
          supposedly natural infidelity of women. There is also the
          Wife of Bath's favourite theme of female mastery.
979   *pine*, pain.
982–5   M.

990   M; *forthink*, are sorry for.

994–1003 M.

994   *minnie*, mother.

1003   *shapes*, means.

1005–7   Spoken by TAILOR'S WIFE in Kemp's version.

In dreid ye be miscarryt!

CHASTITY *now goes to the end of the stage where the* COMMON
PEOPLE *are watching. She approaches* SOUTAR *and* TAILOR, *near
whom are* SOUTAR'S WIFE, TAILOR'S WIFE, *and* JENNIE, *the
tailor's daughter.*

CHASTITY: Ye men of craft, of great ingine,
  Give me harbry for Christis pine,
  And win God's benison, and mine,   980
    And help my hungry heart!
SOUTAR: Welcome, by Him that made the moon,
  To dwell with us till it be June.
  We sall mend baith your hose and shoon,
    And plainly tak your part.
TAILOR: Is this fair Lady Chastity?
  Now welcome by the Trinity!
  I think it were a great pity
    That thou sould lie thereout!
  Your great displeasure we forthink.   990
  Sit doun, Madame, and tak a drink,
  And let na sorrow in you sink,
    But let us play cap-out.
  They entertain CHASTITY.
JENNIE: Ho! Minnie, minnie, minnie!
TAILOR'S WIFE: What wald thou, my dear dochter, Jennie?
  Jennie, my joy, where is thy daddy?
JENNIE: Marry, drinkand with a lusty lady,
  A fair young maiden cled in white,
  Of whom my daddy taks delight.
  She has the fairest form of face,   1000
  Furnisht with all kind of grace.
  I traist, if I can reckon richt,
  She shapes to ludge with him all nicht!
SOUTAR'S WIFE: What does the Soutar, my goodman?
JENNIE: Marry, fills the cup and tooms the can.
  Or ye come hame, by God, I trow
  He will be drucken like a sow!

1009   *cow-clink*, whore.

1011   *cummer*, gossip.

1011–15 First speech given to Soutar's Wife, second to Taylor's Wife, in Kemp.

1012   *ding*, beat.

1014   *smaiks*, wretches.

1015   *paiks*, punishment.

1017   *but*, without.

1019   *rock*, distaff.

1020   *dudron*, slut.

1021   *Sant Blaise*, a Cappadocian bishop, after a hermit's life martyred by Diocletian.

1022–3   Spoken by Soutar's wife in Kemp.

1024–5   M.

1026   *Sant Crispinane*. Saint Crispin was the patron saint of cobblers.

1027   *gane*, mouth.

1031   *harn-pan*, skull.

TAILOR'S WIFE: This is a great despite, I think,
  For to resaive sic a cow-clink.
  What is your counsel that we do?   1010
SOUTAR'S WIFE: Cummer, this is my counsel, lo:
  Ding ye the tane, and I the other.
TAILOR'S WIFE: I am content, by God's Mother!
  I think for me, thae hureson smaiks,
  They serve richt weill to get their paiks!
  They drive CHASTITY *away.*
TAILOR'S WIFE: Go hence, harlot, how durst thou be sa bauld
  To ludge with our goodmen but our licence?
  I mak a vow by Him that Judas sauld,
  This rock of mine shall be thy recompence!
  Shaw me thy name, dudron, with diligence!   1020
CHASTITY: Marry, Chastity is my name, by Sant Blaise.
TAILOR'S WIFE: I pray God may He work on thee vengeance,
  For I luvit never chastity all my days!
  She pursues CHASTITY *with her distaff, then the* WIVES *turn on
  their husbands.*
SOUTAR'S WIFE: But my goodman, the truth I say thee till,
  Gars me keep chastity, sair agains my will.
  I mak a vow to Sant Crispinane
  I'se be revengit on that graceless gane.
  And to begin the play, tak there a platt!
  She strikes the SOUTAR.
SOUTAR: The fiend resaive the hands that gave me that!
SOUTAR'S WIFE: What now, hureson, begins thou for to ban?
  Tak there another upon thy peeled harn-pan!   1031
  (*to* TAILOR'S WIFE) What now, cummer, will thou nocht
  tak a part?
TAILOR'S WIFE: That sall I do, cummer, with all my heart.
  As the WIVES *chase their husbands off,* SOLACE *catches sight of*
  CHASTITY *and speaks to the* KING.
SOLACE: Sovereign, get up and see a heavenly sicht,
  A fair lady in white abilyement!
  She may be peer unto a king or knicht,

1052   *dispone*, dispose of.

1055   *flemit*, banished.

1058   *duleful*, painful.

Maist like an angel by my judgëment!
The KING *rises from among the ladies.*
KING: I sall gang see that sicht incontinent,
  (*to* SENSUALITY) Madame, behauld if ye have knawledging
  Of yon lady, or what is her intent.   1041
  Thereefter we sall turn but tarrying.
SENSUALITY: Sir, let me see what yon matter may mean –
  Perchance that I may knaw her by her face.
  She looks more closely at CHASTITY.
  But doubt this is Dame Chastity, I ween!
  Sir, I and she cannot bide in ane place!
  But if it be the pleasure of your grace,
  That I remain into your company,
  This woman richt hastily gar chase,
  That she na mair be seen in this country!   1050
KING: As ever ye please, sweetheart, sa sall it be!
  Dispone her as ye think expedient.
  Even as ye list to let her live or die,
  I will refer to you that judgëment.
SENSUALITY: I will that she be flemit incontinent,
  And never to come again in this country;
  And if she does, but doubt she sall repent,
  As als perchance a duleful deid sall die!
  Pass on, Sir Sapience and Discretioun,
  And banis her out of the King's presence!   1060
DECEIT: That sall we do, Madame, by God's passioun!
  We sall do your command with diligence,
  And at your hand serve goodly recompense.
  Dame Chastity, come on, be not aghast!
  We sall richt soon, upon your awn expense,
  Into the stocks your bonny foot mak fast!
  The VICES *place* CHASTITY *in the stocks beside* VERITY.
CHASTITY: Sister, alas, this is a care-full case,
  That we with princes sould be sa abhorred!
VERITY: Be blithe, sister, I trust within short space,
  That we sall be richt honourably restored,   1070

1077   *dress*, prepare.

1093   *mangit*, mad.

And with the King we sall be at concord,
For I hear tell Divine Correctioun
Is new landit, thankit be Christ our Lord!
I wot he will be our protectioun!
A fanfare. Enter CORRECTION'S VARLET.
VARLET: Sirs, stand back and hauld you coy.
I am the King Correctioun's boy,
  Come here to dress his place!
See that ye mak obedience
Unto his noble excellence
  Fra time ye see his face!   1080
For he maks reformatiouns
Out-through all Christian natiouns,
  Where he finds great debates.
And sa far as I understand,
He sall reform into this land
  Even all the Three Estates.
For silence I protest
  Baith of Lord, Laird and Leddy!
Now will I rin but rest
  And tell that all is reddy!   1090
Another fanfare. Exit CORRECTION'S VARLET. *The* THREE
VICES *go into conference.*
DECEIT: Brother, hear ye yon proclamatioun?
I dreid full sair of reformatioun.
  Yon message maks me mangit!
What is your counsel, to me tell.
Remain we here, by God himsell,
  We will be all three hangit!
FLATTERY: I'll gang to Spirituality
And preach out-through his diocie,
  Where I will be unknawn,
Or keep me close into some closter   1100
With mony piteous Paternoster,
  Till all thir blasts be blawn.
DECEIT: I'll be weill treatit, as ye ken,

85

1115   Deceit, it will be remembered, had been made the King's
           Treasurer.

1124   *landwart,* country.

With my maisters, the Merchant men,
   Whilk can mak small debate;
Ye ken richt few of them that thrives
Or can beguile the landwart wives,
   But me their man Deceit.
Now, Falset, what sall be thy shift?
FALSET: Na, care thou not, man, for my thrift!   1110
   Trows thou that I be daft?
Na, I will live a lusty life,
Withouten ony sturt or strife,
   Amang the men of craft.
DECEIT: Falset, I wald we made a band –
Now, while the King is yet sleepand
   What rack to steal his box?
FALSET: Now, weill said by the Sacrament!
I sall it steal incontinent,
   Thocht it had twenty locks!   1120
FALSET *steals the* KING'S *box.*
Lo, here the box! Now let us ga,
This may suffice for our rewairds!
DECEIT: Yea, that it may, man, by this day!
It may weill mak us landwart lairds!
Now let us cast away our clais,
In dreid some follow on the chase!
FALSET: Richt weill devisit, by Sant Blaise.
Wald God we were out of this place!
Here they cast away their disguises.
DECEIT: Now, sen there is na man to wrang us,
I pray you, brother, with my heart,   1130
Let us ga part this pelf amang us,
Syne hastily we sall depart!
FALSET: Trows thou to get as mekle as I?
That sall thou not! I stall the box!
Thou did nathing but lookit by,
Ay lurkand like a wily fox!

1138   *craig*, neck.

1139-41   *Rex . . . gloriae*, 'O King of fearful majesty, O strict judge of vengeance, Omnipotent King of glory'. The Latin lines are from the hymn, 'Dies irae, dies illa'.

1152   *weir*, war.
1153   *bud*, bribe; *owrsile*, deceive.

1157   *cankert*, corrupt.

DECEIT *and* FALSET *fight.*

FALSET: Alas for ever my eye is out!

DECEIT: Upon thy craig tak there a clout!

> FLATTERY *has meantime stolen the box and runs out pursued by*
> DECEIT *and* FALSEHOOD. *Their flight is hastened by the fanfare*
> *and stately march to which enter* DIVINE CORRECTION *and his*
> *train. The* ESTATES *sing.*
>
> *Rex tremendae majestatis,*
> *Juste judex ultionis,* 1140
> *Rex omnipotens gloriae.*

CORRECTION: I am callit Divine Correctioun.
Where I am nocht is na tranquillity.
By me traitors and tyrants are put doun,
Wha thinks na shame of their iniquity.
What is a King? Nocht but an officer,
To cause his lieges live in equity,
And under God to be a punisher
Or trespassers against His Majesty.
I am a judge, richt potent and seveir, 1150
Come to do justice mony thousand mile.
I am sa constant, baith in peace and weir,
Na bud nor favour may my sicht owrsile.

> GOOD COUNSEL *enters and runs to greet his master.*

GOOD COUNSEL: Welcome, my lord, welcome ten thousand
        times
To all faithful and true men of this regioun!
Welcome for to correct all faults and crimes
Amang this cankert congregatioun!
Loose Chastity, I mak supplicatioun,
Put to freedom fair Lady Verity,
Wha by unfaithful folk of this natioun 1160
Lies bound full fast into captivity!

CORRECTION: I marvel, Good Counsel, how that may be –
Are ye nocht with the King familiar?

GOOD COUNSEL: That am I nocht, my lord, full wae is me,
But like a beggar am haulden at the bar.

1167   *disguisit,* transformed.

1169   *supprisit,* oppressed.

1173   *do but mocks,* only make game.

1181   M.

1185   *stand ford,* warrant.

1195   *eneuch,* enough.

CORRECTION: Where lies yon ladies in captivity?
  He turns to VERITY *and* CHASTITY *in the stocks.*
  How now, sisters, wha has you sa disguisit?
VERITY: Unfaithful members of iniquity
  Despitefully, my lord, has us supprisit.
CORRECTION: Ga, put yon ladies to their liberty   1170
  Incontinent, and break doun all the stocks!
  But doubt, they are full dear welcome to me!
  Mak diligence! Methinks ye do but mocks!
  Speed hand, and spare not for to break the locks,
  And tenderly tak them up by the hand!
  Had I them here, these knaves sould ken my knocks,
  That them oppresst and banist of this land!
  Members of CORRECTION'S *retinue release* VERITY *and* CHAS-
  TITY. *The* COURTIERS *spy* CORRECTION.
WANTONNESS: Solace, knaws thou not what I see?
  A knicht, or else a king thinks me.
    Brother, what may this mean?   1180
  I understand not by this day
  Wheder that he be freind or fae!
  Stand still and hear what he will say.
    Sic ane I have not seen!
SOLACE: Yon is a stranger I stand ford.
  He seems to be a lusty lord.
PLACEBO: I rede us, put upon the King,
  And wauken him of his sleeping!
  He rouses the KING *from the arms of* SENSUALITY.
  Sir, rise and see an uncouth thing!
    Get up, ye lie too lang!   1190
SENSUALITY: Put on your hood, John-fool! Ye rave!
  How dare you be so pert, Sir Knave,
  To touch the King? Sa Christ me save,
    False hureson, thou sall hang!
  CORRECTION *approaches the* KING.
CORRECTION: Get up, Sir King, ye have sleepit eneuch
  Into the arms of Lady Sensual!

1197-8   M.

1199   *Noy*, Noah.

1211   *doun-thring*, throw down.

1218   *dilatioun*, delay.

1228   *air*, early.

The KING *rises and faces him.*
Be sure that mair belangis to the pleuch,
As efterwart, perchance, rehearse I sall.
Remember how, into the time of Noy
For the foul stink and sin of lechery,   1200
God by my wand did all the warld destroy.
Sodom and Gomore richt sa full rigorously
For that vile sin were brunt maist cruelly.
Therefore I thee command incontinent,
Banish from thee that hure, Sensuality,
Or else but doubt rudely thou sall repent!
KING: By whom have ye sa great authority?
  Wha does presume for to correct a King?
  Knaw ye nocht me, great King Humanity,
  That in my regioun royally does ring?   1210
CORRECTION: I have power great princes to doun-thring
  That lives contrair the Majesty Divine,
  Against the truth whilk plainly does maling;
  Repent they nocht, I put them to ruine.
  I will begin at thee, whilk is the heid,
  And mak on thee first reformatioun,
  Thy lieges than will follow thee but pleid!
  Swith, harlot, hence without dilatioun!
SENSUALITY: My lord, I mak you supplicatioun,
  Give me licence to pass again to Rome!   1220
  Amang the princes of that natioun,
  I let you wit my fresh beauty will bloom!
  Adieu, Sir King, I may na langer tarry!
  I care nocht that. As good luve comes as gaes!
  I recommend you to the Queen of Faerie.
  I see ye will be guidit by my faes!
SENSUALITY *and her retinue pass to the* ESTATE SPIRITUAL.
  My lordis of the Spritual State,
  Venus preserve you air and late!
  For I can mak na mair debate,
    I am partit with your king,   1230

1238   Lindsay's stage direction reads, 'Heir sal the Bishops, Abbots and Persons kis the Ladies'.

1262   *dress*, settle.

And am banist this regioun,
By council of Correctioun.
Be ye nocht my protectioun,
    I may seek my ludging!
BISHOP: Welcome, our days' darling!
    Welcome with all our heart!
    We all but feignyeing
    Sall plainly tak your part!
    BISHOP, ABBOT *and* PARSON *kiss the ladies, who then take their*
    places with them. CORRECTION *returns to the* KING.
CORRECTION: Sen ye are quit of Sensuality,
    Resave into your service Good Counsel,   1240
    And richt sa this fair Lady Chastity
    Till ye marry some Queen of blood royal.
    Observe then chastity matrimonial.
    Richt sa resave Verity by the hand.
    Use their counsel, your fame sall never fall.
    With them therefore, mak a perpetual band!
    The KING *receives* GOOD COUNSEL, CHASTITY *and* VERITY.
    Now, sir, tak tent what I will say,
    Observe thir same baith nicht and day,
    And let them never part you fra,
        Or else withouten doubt,   1250
    Turn ye to Sensuality,
    To vicious life and ribaldry,
    Out of your realm richt shamefully
        Ye sall be rootit out!
KING: I am content to your counsel t'incline.
    At your command sall be all that is mine.
    Solemn music. He embraces CORRECTION.
CORRECTION: I counsel you incontinent
    To gar proclaim a Parliament
        Of all the Three Estates,
    That they be here with diligence   1260
    To mak to you obedience
        And syne dress all debates!

1269   *compeir*, appear when summoned.

1273   *underlie*, suffer.

1279   *denier*, penny.

1285   *the teind . . . Mire*. The texts read 'Ferry Mire.' Hamer identifies
the allusion to Ferny Mire – place-names in this area are also
spelled 'Ferry' – a bog beside Lindsay's estate at Mount Hill
in Monimail Parish, Fife. The jest lies in the non-existence of
the said mussels. Lindsay, like Diligence, was a herald.
Compare the complaint of SOLACE at ll. 115–21, and the
Scribe's sudden interruption of the dialogue at l. 2077 to
complain of unpaid services.

1289   *the coal-pots of Tranent*, the coal-pits of Tranent in Haddington-
shire.

1291   *drouth*, thirst.

1293   *ocht*, aught.

KING: That sall be done, but mair demand.
   Ho, Diligence, come here fra-hand
      And tak your informatioun.
   Go, warn the Spirituality,
   Richt sa the Temporality,
      By open proclamatioun,
   In goodly haste for to compeir
   In their most honourable maneir   1270
      To give us their counsails!
   Wha that beis absent, to them shaw
   That they sall underlie the Law
      And punist be that fails!
DILIGENCE: Sir, I sall baith in borough and land,
   With diligence do your command,
      Upon my awn expense.
   Sir, I have servit you all this year,
   But I gat never a denier
      Yet for my recompense!   1280
KING: Pass on, and thou sall be regairdit
   And for thy service weill rewairdit,
      For-why, with my consent,
   Thou sall have yearly for thy hire
   The teind mussels of the Ferry Mire
      Confirmt in Parliament.
DILIGENCE: I will get riches through that rent
      Efter the day of Doom,
   When in the coal-pots of Tranent
      Butter will grow on broom!   1290
   All nicht I had sa meikle drouth,
      I micht not sleep a wink.
   Or I proclaim ocht with my mouth,
      But doubt I mon have drink!
   While DILIGENCE *refreshes himself* DIVINE CORRECTION
   tackles the COURTIERS.
CORRECTION: Come here, Placebo and Solace,
   With your companion Wantonness,

1308   *remissioun*, pardon.

1310   *tables*, backgammon.

1327–8   M.
1328   *waur*, worse.

1331   *whilk*, that.

I knaw weill your conditioun.
For ticeting King Humanity
To resave Sensuality
Ye mon suffer punitioun! 1300
WANTONNESS: We grant, my Lord, we have done ill;
Therefore we put us in your will,
But we have been abusit!
PLACEBO: For in good faith, sir, we believit
That lechery had na man grievit
Because it is sa usit!
SOLACE: Sir, we sall mend our conditioun
Sa ye give us remissioun.
But give us leave to sing,
To dance, to play at chess and tables, 1310
To read stories and merry fables
For pleasure of our King!
CORRECTION: Sa that ye do na other crime,
Ye sall be pardont at this time,
For-why, as I suppose,
Princes may sometime seek solace
With mirth and lawful merriness,
Their spirits to rejose.
And richt sa hawking and hunting
Are honest pastimes for a king, 1320
Into the time of peace;
And learn to rin a heavy spear,
That he into the time of weir
May follow at the chase.
KING: Where is Sapience and Discretioun?
And why comes not Devotioun near?
VERITY: Sapience, sir, was a very loon,
And Devotioun was nine times waur.
CHASTITY: They three were Flattery and Deceit,
And Falset, that unhappy loon, 1330
Against us three whilk made debate
And banist us fra toun to toun.

1333 *soun*, swoon.

1338 *Sant Fillane*, an eighth-century Scots saint after whom Strath-fillan is named. He had the special prayers of Bruce before Bannockburn.

1339 *paiks*, punishment.

1340 *playit me the glaiks*, made a fool of me.

They gart us twa fall into soun,
When they us lockit in the stocks.
That dastart knave, Discretioun,
Full theftuously did steal your box!

KING: The Deil tak them, sen they are gane!
I mak a vow to sweet Sant Fillane,
Get I them they sall beir their paiks.
I see they have playit me the glaiks!   1340
Good Counsel, now shaw me the best.
How sall I keep my realm in rest?

GOOD COUNSEL: The principal point, sir, of a king's office,
Is for to do to every man justice,
And for to mix his justice with mercy,
But rigour, favour or partiality.
Wha guides them weill, they win immortal fame;
Wha the contrair, they get perpetual shame.
The Chronicles to knaw, I you exhort;
There sall ye find baith good and evil report;   1350
For every prince efter his quality,
Thocht he be deid his deeds sall never die!
Sir, if ye please for to use my counsel,
Your fame and name sall be perpetual.
A fanfare.

DILIGENCE: Hoyez, hoyez, hoyez!
At the command of King Humanity,
I warn and charge all members of Parliament,
Baith Spiritual State and Temporality,
That to his grace they be obedient
And speed them to the court, incontinent,   1360
In good order, arrayit royally.
Wha beis absent or inobedient,
The King's displeasure they sall underlie!
To the audience.
And als I mak you exhortatioun,
Sen ye have heard the first part of our play,
Go, tak a drink, and mak collatioun;

101

1371   *ingine,* mind.

Ilk man drink to his marrow, I you pray.
Tarry nocht lang, it is late in the day.
Let some drink ale, and some drink claret wine;
By great doctors of physic I hear say   1370
That michty drink comforts the dull ingine!
Music, a march. All go off.

END OF PART ONE

1372	The interlude of the Poor Man and the Pardoner is to be considered integral to the play for its illustration of one aspect of the corrupting influence of Flattery on the Church. As a friar he has not only encouraged the hierarchy to leave the duty of preaching to him, but here destroys its credit with his unscrupulous exploitation of selfishly motivated superstitions. In the 1554 Quarto the interlude is preceded by the statement: 'thair is to cum, I say you / The best pairt of our Play. / The END of the first part of the SATYRE. / Now sall the pepill mak Collatioun, then beginnis the Interlude, the Kings, Bischops and principall players being out of their seats'. The principal players have not left because the interlude is mere pastime but because they must soon re-enter at its close, 'gangand backwart'.
1375	*wiss*, direct
1378-9	M.
1378	*faillies*, faults.
1379	*Provost and Baillies*. These officials (English equivalent mayor and aldermen) would be in the audience.
1383	*brunt shins*, able limbs. The shin is the forepart of the leg between knee and ankle; in this context 'brunt' seems to have meant 'forward', 'active'. John mimics the kind of oath that courtiers affected.
1388	*crookit*, lame.
1389	*meikle*, great.

PART TWO

Fanfare. DILIGENCE *comes on to the empty stage as if to make a proclamation. Before he can do so, the* POOR MAN *enters, addressing the audience.*

POOR MAN: Of your almous, good folks, for God's love of
  heaven,
 For I have motherless bairnis either sax or seven!
 If ye will give na good, for luve of sweet Jesus,
 Wiss me the richt way to Sant Andrews.
DILIGENCE: Where have we gotten this goodly companion?
 Swith! Furth of the field, thou false, raggit loon!
 Fie on you officers that mends not thir faillies!
 I give you all to the Deil, baith Provost and Baillies.
 Without ye come and chase this carl away   1380
 The deil a word ye's get mair of our play!
 The POOR MAN *climbs on to the* KING's *throne.*
 Come doun, or by God's croun, false loon I sall slay thee!
POOR MAN: Now sweir by thy brunt shins, the Deil ding them
  fra thee!
DILIGENCE: Swith! Beggar bogle, haste thee away,
 Thou art over pert to spoil our play!
POOR MAN: I will not give for all your play worth a sow's fart,
 For there is richt little play at my hungry heart!
DILIGENCE: What deil ails this crookit carl?
POOR MAN: Marry, meikle sorrow!
 I cannot get, thocht I gasp, to beg nor to borrow.   1390
DILIGENCE: Where, deil, is this thou dwells, or what is thine
  intent?
POOR MAN: I dwell into Lothian, a mile fra Tranent.
DILIGENCE: Where wald thou be, carl? The sooth to me shaw!
POOR MAN: Sir, even to Sant Andrews, for to seek law.
DILIGENCE: For to seek law, in Edinburgh is the nearest way.
POOR MAN: Sir, I socht law there this mony dear day;

1397   *Session.* The College of Justice, the supreme civil court, was only instituted in 1532, but similar courts had functioned since the reign of James I.

            Senyie. A consistory or diocesan court had jurisdiction over such causes as tithes, testaments, matrimonial and heretical affairs. The Poor Man has been unsuccessful in his plea to the inferior consistory at Edinburgh and now wishes to appeal to the senior diocesan court at St Andrews. The priest's funerary exactions of the '*cors*present' of a cow, or clothing, like the landlord's 'herild' (i.e. 'lord's due') of a horse or cow, was not exceptional but customary practice. Lindsay's play doubtless influenced the decision of a Church Council in 1559 to mitigate such exactions in the case of the very poor.

1407   *meir*, mare.

1409   *fat*, well fleshed.

1410   *tidier*, plumper.

1412   *mane*, lament.

1415   *baitand*, grazing.

1416   *hereild* (see note to l. 1397).

1424   *cleikit*, seized.

1425   *umest clais*, 'uppermost clothing', i.e. the bed covering?

            rapploch, homespun

But I could get nane at Session or Senyie,
Therefore the meikle dumb deil droun all that menyie!
DILIGENCE Shaw me thy matter, man, with all the circumstance,
How thou has happent this unhappy chance.   1400
POOR MAN: Good man, will ye give me of your charity
And I sall declare you the black verity.
My father was an auld man and a hair
And was of age four score of years and mair,
And Maud my mother was four score and fiftein;
And with my labour I did them baith sustein.
We had a meir that carriet salt and coal,
And everilk year she brocht us hame a foal.
We had three kye that was baith fat and fair,
Nane tidier into the toun of Ayr.   1410
My father was sa weak of bluid and bane,
That he deit, wherefore my mother made great mane.
Then she deit within a day or two,
And there began my poverty and woe.
Our good grey meir was baitand on the field
And our land's laird took her for his hereild.
Our vicar took the best cow by the heid
Incontinent, when my father was deid.
And when the vicar heard tell how that my mother
Was deid, fra-hand he took fra me another.   1420
Then Meg my wife did murn baith even and morrow
Till at the last she deit for very sorrow.
And when the vicar heard tell my wife was deid,
The thrid cow he cleikit by the heid.
Their umest clais, that were of rapploch grey,
The vicar gart his clerk beir them away.
When all was gane I micht mak na debate,
But with my bairns passed for to beg my meat.
Now I have tauld you the black verity
How I am brocht into this misery.   1430

1431   *the Parson.* The vicar held his benefice *in cure* for a religious house, abbey or nunnery; the parson was responsible for the whole parish'.

1432   *teind*, tithe.

1434   *Pace*, Easter.

1436   *Inglis groat*, also known as the 'silver penny'.

1452   *Rome-raker*, anyone travelling to Rome for religious reasons, but here one who goes there for motives of greed, to obtain a benefice or pardoner's license. Lindsay makes fun of the title, 'Sir', that gave priests the comic description of 'Pope's Knights' (see 1450).

1456   *privilege*, license.

DILIGENCE: How did the Parson? Was he not thy good freind?

POOR MAN: The Deil stick him! He curst me for my teind
 And haulds me yet under that same process,
 That gart me want the Sacrament at Pace.
 In good faith, sir, thocht ye wald cut my throat,
 I have na gear except ane Inglis groat
 Whilk I purpose to give a man of law.

DILIGENCE: Thou art the daftest fool that ever I saw!
 Trows thou, man, by the law to get remeid
 Of men of Kirk? Na, never till thou be deid!   1440
 Be sure of priests thou will get na support.

POOR MAN: If that be true, the fiend resave the sort!
 Sa, sen I see I get na other grace,
 I will lie down and rest me in this place.

He does so. Enter PARDONER, *who is* FLATTERY *in his disguise.*

PARDONER: *Bona dies, bona dies!*
 Devote people, good day I say you,
 Now tarry a little while I pray you
  Till I be with you knawn!
 Wot ye weill how I am namit?
 A noble man and undefamit,   1450
  If all the sooth were shawn.
 I am Sir Robert Rome-raker,
 A perfite public pardoner
  Admittit by the Paip.
 Sirs, I sall shaw you, for my wage,
 My pardons and my privilege,
  Whilk ye sall see and graip.
 I give to the Deil with good intent
 This waeful wickit New Testament,
  With them that it translatit!   1460
 Since laymen knew the verity,
 Pardoners gets na charity
  Without that they debate it.
 Deil fell the brain that has it wrocht,
 Sa fall them that the Book hame brocht!

1468   *Black Bullenger and Melancthoun.* Heinrich Bullinger (1504–75), the Swiss Reformer; Philip Melancthon (1497–1560), the German Reformer, who assisted Luther in his translation of the New Testament.

1469   *smoored*, smothered; *cude*, baptismal face-cloth.

1471   *Sant Paul* is cursed because his Epistles were a favourite authority of the Reformers for their criticisms of the Church.

1474   *into: the mirk.* in the dark, i.e. secretly

1477   *Cam of Tartary*, the Khan of Tartary, a comic name for the Devil.

1478   *oyster-shells.* The cockle or scallop shell was the badge of a pilgrim.

1483   *Finn Macoul.* A hero of Irish legend credited with giant strength.

1483   *chaft-blade*, cheek-bone.

1486–7   *Mac Connels corn . . . Bawhidder.* The allusion has not been identified. Balquhidder is a village in West Perthshire.

1489   *Johnnie Armistrang*, John Armstrong, a celebrated Border reiver hanged by James V. See the ballad of Johnnie Armstrang.

Als I pray to the Rood,
That Martin Luther, that false loon,
Black Bullenger and Melancthoun,
    Had been smoored in their cude!
By him that bure the croun of thorn   1470
I wald Sant Paul had never been born,
    And als I wald his books
Were never read into the Kirk,
But amang freirs into the mirk,
    Or riven amang the rooks!
My patent pardons ye may see,
Come from the Cam of Tartary
    Weill sealt with oyster shells.
Thocht ye have na contritioun
Ye sall have full remissioun   1480
    With help of books and bells.
Here is a relic, lang and braid,
Of Finn Macoul the richt chaft-blade,
    With teeth and all together.
Of Colin's cow here is a horn,
For eating of MacConnel's corn
Was slain into Bawhidder.
Here is a cord baith great and lang,
Whilk hangit Johnnie Armistrang,
    Of good hemp saft and sound.   1490
Good haily people, I stand ford,
Whaever beis hangit with this cord
    Needs never to be dround!
Come win the pardon, now let see,
For meal, for malt or for money,
    For cock, hen, goose, or grice!
Of relics here I have a hunder.
Why come ye not? This is a wonder.

1499   NOTE: part of the interlude is omitted here; the Pardoner acts as a devil's priest in an obscenely performed ceremony of divorce between a cobbler and his wife. He claims that his 'pardon' can save them from the hell of unhappy marriage. S.D. Wilkin does not appear in Kemp's version.

1500–23   M.

1501   *Widdiefow*. The surname means 'gallows-bird'.

1513–1518 *Christian Anderson . . . Bawburd*, a reference to whores.

1515   *limmer*, rascal.

1524   *crack*, brag.

1526   *sain*, bless.

1527   *Sant Bride . . . again!* Saint Bridget, the Irish saint, is remembered here particularly for the legend of her recovery of some stolen cattle.

          I trow ye be not wise!
     The PARDONER'S BOY, WILKIN *is heard calling.*
WILKIN: Ho, maister, ho, where are ye now?   1500
PARDONER: I am here, Wilkin Widdiefow.
WILKIN: Sir, I have done your bidding,
     For I have fund a great horse-bane,
     A fairer saw ye never nane,
     Upon Tom Flesher's midden.
     Sir, ye may gar the wifeis trow
     It is a bane of Sant Bride's cow,
          Good for the fever quartane.
     Sir, will ye rule this relic weill,
     All haill the wives will kiss and kneel,   1510
          Betwix this and Dumbartane.
PARDONER: Where sall I ludge into the toun?
WILKIN: With good kind Christian Andersoun,
          Where ye will be weill treatit.
     If ony limmer you demands,
     She will defend you with her hands
          And womanly debate it.
     Bawburd says, by the Trinity,
     That she sall beir you company,
          Howbeit ye bide a year.   1520
PARDONER: Thou has done weill, by God's mother!
     Tak ye the tane and I the tother,
          Sa sall we mak great cheer.
     The POOR MAN *wakes up.*
POOR MAN: What thing was yon that I heard crack and cry?
     I have been dreamand and drivelland of my kye!
     With my richt hand my haill body I sain,
     Sant Bride, Sant Bride, send me my kye again!
     He sees the PARDONER.
     I see standand yonder a haily man.
     To mak me help, let me see if he can!
     Haily maister, God speed you and good morn.   1530

1531   *at the horn*, outlawed. Outlawry was proclaimed by horn or trumpet at the market-cross of the head burgh of the outlaw's district.

1537   *fra-hand*, forthwith.
1538   *lost*, damned.

1543   *ripe*, search.

1551   *pleid*, plea.

1561   *but weir*, doubtless.

PARDONER: Welcome to me thocht thou were at the horn.
Come win the pardon, and then I sall thee sain!
POOR MAN: Will that pardon get me my kye again?
PARDONER: Carl, of thy kye I have nathing ado.
Come win my pardon, and kiss my relics too.
He blesses him with his relics.
Now loose thy purse, and lay doun thy offrand,
And thou sall have my pardon even fra-hand.
Now win the pardon, limmer, or thou art lost!
POOR MAN: My haily father, what will that pardon cost?
PARDONER: Let see what money thou beiris in thy bag.   1540
POOR MAN: I have ae groat here bund into a rag.
PARDONER: Hast thou na other siller but a groat?
POOR MAN: If I have mair, sir, come and ripe my coat!
PARDONER: Give me that groat, man, if thou has na mair.
POOR MAN: With all my heart, maister, lo, tak it, there!
Now let me see your pardon, with your leave.
PARDONER: A thousand year of pardons I thee give!
POOR MAN: A thousand year? I will not live sa lang.
Deliver me it, maister, and let me gang!
PARDONER: A thousand year I lay upon thy heid,   1550
With *totiens quotiens;* now mak me na mair pleid.
Thou hast resavit thy pardon now already.
POOR MAN: But I can see nathing, sir, by our Lady!
PARDONER: What craves the carl? Methinks thou art not wise!
POOR MAN: I crave my groat, or else my merchandise!
PARDONER: I gave thee pardon for a thousand year!
POOR MAN: How sall I get that pardon? Let me hear!
PARDONER: Stand still, and I sall tell thee the haill story!
When thou art deid and gaes to Purgatory,
Being condemnt to pain a thousand year,   1560
Then sall thy pardon thee relieve but weir!
Now be content! Ye are a mervellous man!
POOR MAN: Sall I get nathing for my groat till then?
PARDONER: That sall thou not! I mak it to you plain!

1568   *steid*, place.

1576-9 M. *abet*, abate, lessen.
1577   *het*, heat.

1579   *dryte*, make dirt; *gambs*, tricks.
1580   *mangit*, mad.

1583   *rout*, blow.

1594   *by adulatioun*, without flattery; 'without any' is a frequent
        sense of 'by'.

The poor man is now very angry.

POOR MAN: Na? Then, gossip, give me my groat again!
  What say ye, maisters? Call ye this good reason,
  That he sould promise me a good pardon,
  And here resave my money in this steid,
  Syne mak me na payment till I be deid?
  When I am deid, I wot full sickerly   1570
  My silly saul will pass to Purgatory.
  Declare me this! Now God nor Belial bind thee,
  When I am there, curst carl, where sall I find thee?
  Not into heaven, but rather into hell!
  When thou art there, thou cannot help thysell!
  When will thou come my dolours to abet?
  Or I thee find my hips will get a het!
  Trows thou, butcher, that I will buy blind lambs?
  Give me my groat! The Deil dryte on thy gambs!
PARDONER: Swith! Stand aback! I trow this man be   1580
     mangit!
  Thou gets not this, carl, thocht thou sould be hangit!
POOR MAN: Give me my groat, weill bund into a clout!
  Or by God's breid, Robin sall beir a rout!
He sets upon the PARDONER, scatters his relics and chases him off.
DILIGENCE: What kind of daffing is this all day?
  Swith, smaiks, out of the field, away!
  Into a prison put them soon,
  Syne hang them when the play is done!
*A fanfare and a march. Enter the KING, his COURTIERS, DIVINE
CORRECTION, the VIRTUES. The music continues with the speech.*
  Famous people, tak tent, and ye sall see
  The Three Estatis of this natioun,
  Come to the court with a strange gravity.   1590
  Therefore I mak you supplicatioun,
  Till ye have heard our haill narratioun
  To keep silence and be patient I pray you.
  Howbeit we speak by adulatioun

117

1595   As appears from ll. 1708–23, the spiritual Estate is led by the figures of Covetice and Sensuality, the temporal Estate by that of Public Oppression, and the Burgesses by those of Falset and Deceit. Flattery, though first identified with the Court and now protected by Spirituality, belongs everywhere.

1606   *mon*, must.

1625   *heids*, leaders.

We sall say nathing but the sooth, I say you!
THE THREE ESTATES *enter, led by their* VICES. *They are walking*
backwards, SPIRITUALITY *led by* FLATTERY, COVETICE *and*
SENSUALITY, TEMPORALITY *by* PUBLIC OPPRESSION, *and*
BURGESSES *by* FALSET *and* DECEIT.

WANTONNESS: Now, braid benedicite!
  What thing is yon that I see?
    Look, Solace, my heart!
SOLACE: Brother Wantonness, what thinks thou?
  Yon are the Three Estates, I trow,   1600
  Gangand backwart!
WANTONNESS: Backwart? Backwart? Out wallaway!
  It is great shame for them, I say,
    Backwart to gang.
  I trow the King Correctioun
  Mon mak a reformatioun
    Or it be lang!
  Now let us go and tell the King!
  Sir, we have seen a mervellous thing,
    By our judgment!   1610
  The Three Estates of this regioun
  Are cumand backwart through this toun,
    To the Parliament!
KING: Backwart, backwart, how may that be?
  Gar speed them hastily to me,
    In dreid that they ga wrong!
PLACEBO: Sir, I see them yonder cumand.
  They will be here even fra-hand,
    As fast as they may gang!
GOOD COUNSEL: Sir, hauld you still and scare them not, 1620
  Till you persave what be their thocht,
    And see what men them leids.
  And let the King Correctioun
  Mak a sharp inquisition,
    And mark them by the heids!

1642   *lands*, properties.

1646   *leil*, loyal.

1648   *Ye ... heid*, perhaps the most common of medieval and Renaissance analogies to express the inter-dependence of governor and governed. Lindsay had read the late fifteenth century *Three Tales of The Three Priests of Peebles*, in which a reforming Scots king summons the Three Estates and addresses the Lords thus (11. 105-8):

          Ane heid dow not on body stand allane
          Forout members to be of micht and mane,
          For to uphald the bodie and the heid,
          And sickerlie to gar it stand in steid.

SPIRITUALITY: Gloir, honour, laud, triumph and victory,
Be to your michty prudent excellence.
Here are we come, all the Estatis Three,
Ready to mak our due obedience,
At your command with humble observance,   1630
As may pertein to Sprituality,
With counsel of the Temporality.

TEMPORALITY: Sir, we with michty courage, at command
Of your super-excellent Majesty,
Sall mak service, baith with our heart and hand,
And sall not dreid in thy defence to die.
We are content, but doubt, that we may see
That noble, heavenly King Correctioun,
Sa he with mercy mak punitioun.

BURGESSES: Sir, we are here your Burgesses and Merchants.
Thanks be to God that we may see your face,   1641
Traistand we may now into divers lands
Convoy our gear with support of your grace;
For now, I traist, we sall get rest and peace.
When mis-doers are with your sword owrthrawn,
Then may leil merchants live upon their awn.
The singing ends.

KING: Welcome to me, my prudent lordis all,
Ye are my members, suppose I be your heid.
Sit doun that we may with your just counsel
Agains mis-doers find sovereign remeid.   1650

CORRECTION: My tender freinds, I pray you with my heart,
Declare to me the thing that I wald speir.
What is the cause that ye gang all backwart?
The verity thereof fain wald I hear.

BISHOP: Sovereign, we have gane sa this mony a year.
Howbeit ye think we go undecently,
We think we go richt wonder pleasantly.

DILIGENCE: Sit doun, my lords, into your proper places,

1660   *Dempster*, the officer who pronounced the 'doom' or sentence of the court.

1661   *fence the Court*, formally declare in session. The form of words in a baron court began, 'I defend and biddis in our leige Lord the King's behalfe of Scotland . . . that na man distrouble this court unlawfullie.' (*Habakkuk Bisset's Rolment of Courtis*, Scottish Text Society, note to vol. i, p. 248, l. 10).

1666   *doun-thring*, oppress.

1676   *for-why*, because.

1681   *applyable*, submissive.

1684–5   M.

Syne let the King consider all sic cases.
Sit doun, Sir Scribe, and sit doun Dempster too,　　　1660
And fence the Court as ye were wont to do.
Music as THE ESTATES *take their places and all present dispose*
themselves for a court of enquiry.
KING: My prudent lordis of the Three Estates,
　It is our will, above all other thing,
　For to reform all them that maks debates,
　Contrair the richt whilk daily does maling,
　And they that does the Common-Weal doun-thring.
　With help and counsel of King Correctioun,
　It is our will for to mak punishing,
　And plain oppressors put to subjectioun.
BISHOP: What thing is this, sir, that ye have deviset?　　　1670
　Sirs, ye have need for to be weill adviset.
　Be nocht hasty into your executioun,
　And be not owr extreme in your punitioun.
　And if ye please to do, sir, as we say,
　Postpone this Parliament to another day,
　For-why the people of this regioun
　May nocht endure extreme correctioun!
CORRECTION: Is this the part, my lords, that ye will tak
　To mak us supportatioun to correct?
　It does appear that ye are culpable,　　　1680
　That are not to correctioun applyable!
　Swith, Diligence, ga shaw it is our will,
　That everilk man opprest give in his bill.
DILIGENCE(*proclaims*): All manner of men I warn that be opprest,
　Come and complain and they sall be redrest,
　For-why it is the noble Prince's will
　That ilk complainer sall give in his bill.

1688   JOHN THE COMMONWEAL, had appeared in Lindsay's early
        poem, *The Dreme*, and is here particularly representative of
        the commons, the classes not represented in the Convention
        of the Three Estates, but also more generally of the Scots
        people as distinct from their governors.

1695   *new-made King*. The 1554 Quarto reads 'new-cumde King',
        which should refer to King Correction, but King Humanity
        is intended. He is 'new-crowned', or 'new-made' spiritually.

1702   *crookit*, lame.
1703   *owrlookit*, neglected.

1706   On the Vices that lead the respective Estates see note to l. 1595.
1706   *limmers*, rascals.
1707   *canker colours*, corrupt pretences; *heids*, leaders.

1712-13   M.

JOHN THE COMMON-WEAL, *a sturdy figure, in rags, rushes in. He is seen to be lame.*

JOHN: Out of my gait! For God's sake let me ga!
Tell me again, good maister, what ye say.

DILIGENCE: I warn all that be wrangously offendit,   1690
Come and complain and they sall be amendit.
What is thy name, fellow? That wald I feel.

JOHN: Forsooth, they call me John the Common-Weal.
Good maister, I wald ask at you ane thing –
Where traist ye I sall find yon new-made King?

DILIGENCE: Come owr, and I sall shaw thee to his Grace.
He leads JOHN *to the* KING.

JOHN: God's benison licht on that lucky face!

KING: Shaw me thy name, good man, I thee command.

JOHN: Marry, John the Common-Weal of fair Scotland.
The KING *surveys* JOHN'S *rags*

KING: The Common-Weal has been amang his faes!   1700

JOHN: Yea, sir, that gars the Common-Weal want clais!

KING: What is the cause the Common-Weal is crookit?

JOHN: Because the Common-Weal has been owr-lookit.

KING: What gars thee look sa with a dreary heart?

JOHN: Because the Three Estates gangs all backwart.

KING: Sir Common-Weal, knaw ye the limmers that them leids?

JOHN: Their canker colours, I ken them by the heids:
As for our reverent fathers of Sprituality,
They are led by Covetice, this carl, and Sensuality,
And as ye see, Temporality has need of correctioun,   1710
Whilk has lang time been led by Public Oppressioun.
Lo, where the loon lies lurkand at his back.
Get up! I think to see thy craig gar a raip crack!
Lo, here is Falset and Deceit weill I ken,
Leaders of the Merchants and silly craftsmen.
What mervel thocht the Three Estates backwart gang,
When sic a vile company dwells them amang,
Whilk has rulit this rout mony dear days,
Whilk gars John the Common-Weal want his warm clais?

1720-21	M.
1721	i.e. John would have to become a Border reiver.

1725	*truckers*, rogues.

1728	*pelours*, thieves.

1734	*sweir*, reluctant.

1738	*stewats*, filthy fellows; *brocks*, badgers.

1744-54	The parting speeches of Covetice and Sensuality, along with the Bishop's replies, show what slight expectations Lindsay had of their being separated from the Spiritual Estate.
1744-9	M. Covetice not in Kemp's version.
1748	*Sant Maven*, a Welsh saint who founded the abbey of Saint Meen in Brittany.
1749	*we are twa natural men*, see note to l. 218; they have the same parentage, presumably the Devil.

1752	*dule*, grief.

Sir, call them before you and put them in order,   1720
Or else John the Common-Weal mon beg on the Border!
Thou feignyit Flattery, the fiend fart in thy face!
When ye was guider of the court we gat little grace!
My sovereign Lord Correctioun, I mak you supplicatioun,
Put thir tried truckers from Christ's congregatioun!
CORRECTION: As ye have deviset, but doubt it sall be done!
Come here, my sergeants, and do your debt soon!
Put thir three pelours into prison strang,
Howbeit ye sould hang them, ye do them na wrang!
FIRST SERGEANT: Sovereign lord, we sall obey your commands.
Brother, upon thir limmers lay on your hands!   1731
SECOND SERGEANT: Come here, gossip, come here, come here!
Your reckless life ye sall repent.
When was ye wont to be sa sweir?
Stand still and be obedient!
The SERGEANTS *hustle the* THREE VICES *to the stocks.*
Put in your legs into the stocks,
For ye had never a meeter hose!
Thir stewats stinks as they were brocks!
Now are ye siccar, I suppose!
They go to CORRECTION.
My lord, we have done your commands.   1740
Sall we put Covetice in captivity?
CORRECTION: Yea, heartly lay on them your hands,
Richt sa upon Sensuality!
COVETICE: My reverent fathers tak in patience.
I sall nocht lang remain from your presence.
Thocht for a while I mon from you depart,
I wot my spreit sall remain in your heart.
BISHOP: Adieu, by Sant Maven,
Pass where ye will, we are twa natural men!
SENSUALITY: Adieu, my lord!   1750
BISHOP: Adieu, my awn sweet heart!
Now dule fell me that we twa mon part!
SENSUALITY: My lord, howbeit this parting does me pain,

127

1754   M.

1758   *priset*, approved.

1770   *slaik*, quench; *murmell*, complaint.

1779   *sickerly*, certainly.

I traist in God we sall meet soon again.

THE SERGEANTS *chase* SENSUALITY *and her retinue away to a place among the* POOR PEOPLE *at the foot of the stage.*

LORD: My lords, ye knaw the Three Estates
For Common-Weal sould mak debates.
Let now amang us be deviset
Sic Acts as with good men be priset;
And for to save us fra murmell,
Soon, Diligence, fetch us Good Counsel,   1760
For-why he is a man that knaws
Baith the Canon and Civil Laws.

DILIGENCE *passes to* GOOD COUNSEL.

DILIGENCE: Father, ye mon incontinent
Pass to the Lords of Parliament;
For-why they are determint all
To do nathing but your counsel.

GOOD COUNSEL: My lords, God glad the company!
What is the cause ye send for me?

MERCHANT: Sit doun and give us your counsel,
How we sall slaik the great murmell   1770
Of poor people, that is weill knawn
And as the Common-Weal has shawn.
And als we knaw it is the Kingis will
That good remede be put there-till.
Sir Common-Weal, keep ye the bar.
Let nane except yoursell come near!

JOHN *lays his hand on the* POOR MAN.

JOHN: Ye mon let this poor crëature
Support me for to keep the door.
I knaw his name full sickerly.
He will complain as weill as I.   1780

GOOD COUNSEL: My worthy lords, sen ye have tane on hand
Some reformatioun to mak into this land,
And als ye knaw it is the Kingis mind,
Wha to the Common-Weal has aye been kind,
Thocht reive and thift were stanchit weill eneuch,

1793   *tint*, lost.

1799–1802 M.
1799   *hichtit*, raised; *mail*, rent.
1800   *watter kail*, cabbage soup.

1802   *harlt*, dragged.

1804   *God's breid*, the sacramental bread of Communion.
1805   *nowt*, cattle.

1811   *our ... thieves*, Border reivers, protected by powerful families, raided equally in England and Scotland.
1812   *leil*, loyal.

1821–4   M.

Yet something mair belangis to the pleuch.
Now into peace ye sould provide for weirs,
And be sure of how mony thousand spears
The King may be when he has ocht ado,
For-why, my lords, this is my reason, lo,   1790
The husbandmen and commons they were wont
Go in the battle foremost in the front.
But I have tint all my experience,
Without ye mak some better diligence
The Common-Weal mon other ways be stylet,
Or by my faith the King will be beguilet!
Thir poor commons daily as ye may see
Declinis doun to extreme poverty,
For some are hichtit sa into their mail
Their winning will nocht find them watter kail.   1800
Thus mon they pay great rent or leave the steid,
And some are plainly harlt out by the heid
And are destroyt, without God on them rue!
POOR MAN: Sir, by God's breid, that tale is very true!
  It is weill kend I had baith nowt and horse.
  Now all my gear ye see upon my corse.
CORRECTION: Or I depart I think to mak an order!
JOHN: I pray you, sir, begin first at the Border,
  For how can we fend us agains England,
  When we can not, within our native land,   1810
  Destroy our awn Scots, common traitor thieves,
  Wha to leil labourers daily does mischieves?
  Were I a king, my lord, by Godis wounds,
  Wha-e'er held common thieves within their bounds,
  Where-through that daily leil men micht be wrangt,
  Without remede their chieftains sould be hangt!
LORD: What other enemies has thou, let us ken.
JOHN: Sir, I complain upon the idle men,
  For-why, sir, it is God's awn bidding
  All Christian men to work for their living.   1820
  Sant Paul, that piller of the Kirk,

131

1823   *Qui . . . manducet*, from 2 Thessalonians, iii. 10, is translated in the following line.

1827   *couchers*, wasters.

1828   *quintessencers*, see note to l. 729.

1829   *bable-beirers . . . bards*, fools (with their jester's bauble) and minstrels. They were among the classes discriminated against by the Vagrancy Acts.

1830   *swingeours*, scoundrels.

1831–2   M.

1834   *Augustines, Carmelites and Cordeliers,* monks of the Augustinian, Carmelite and Franciscan Orders.

1848   *Justice ayrs*, assizes.

1849   *pickand, pegrel*, light-fingered, petty.

1854   *compositors*, persons appointed to settle legal disputes.

Says to the wretches that will not work,
Qui non laborat non manducet,
Wha labours nocht he sall not eat.
This been against the strang beggars,
Fiddlers, pipers, and pardoners,
Thir jugglers, jesters and idle couchers,
Thir carriers and thir quintessencers,
Thir bable-beirers and thir bards,
Thir sweir swingeours with lords and lairds,   1830
Mair than their rentis may sustein
Or to their profit needfull been.
This been against thir great fat freirs,
Augustines, Carmelites and Cordeleirs,
And all others that in cowls been cled,
Whilk labours not and been weill fed –
I mean, nocht labourand spiritually,
Nor for their living corporally,
Lyand in dens like idle dogs.
I them compare to weill fed hogs!   1840
I think they do themselves abuse,
Seeing that they the warld refuse;
Having professed sic poverty,
Syne flees fast fra necessity!
CORRECTION: Whom upon mair will ye complain?
JOHN: Marry, on mair and mair again!
For the poor people cries with cares
The misusing of Justice ayrs.
Sic pickand, pegrel thieves are hangt,
But he that all the warld has wrangt,   1850
A cruel tyran, a strang transgressor,
A common public plain oppressor –
By buds may he obtein favours
Of treasurers and compositors,
And through laws, consistorial,
Prolix, corrupt and perpetuall,
The common people are put sa under,

133

1869–78   M.

1879   *pley*, plea.

1885   *give . . . remissioun*. The 'twa' are the Lords and Burgesses, the
        Prelates feeling no need for pardon.

Thocht they be poor, it is na wonder!
CORRECTION: Good John, I grant all that is true.
  Your infortoun full sair I rue!   1860
  Sa, my lord Temporality,
  I you command in time that ye
  Expel Oppressioun aff your lands.
  And als I say to you merchands,
  If ever I find, by land or sea,
  Deceit be in your company,
  Whilk are to Common-weal contrair,
  I vow to God I sall not spare!
  Mairover, my Lord Temporality,
  In goodly haste I will that ye   1870
  Set into feu your temporal lands
  To men that labours with their hands,
  Where-through the policy may incress.
LORD: I am content, sir, by the Mess.
CORRECTION: My Spritual Lords, are ye content?
BISHOP: Na, we mon tak advisëment.
CORRECTION: Conclude ye not with the Common-Weal,
  Ye sall be punisht, by Sant Geil!
  My lords, what say ye to this pley?
LORD: My sovereign lords, we will obey,   1880
  And tak your part with heart and hand,
  Whatever ye please us to command.
  But we beseek you, sovereign,
  Of all our crimes that are by-gane
  To give us twa a full remissioun,
  And here we mak to you conditioun,
  The Common-Weal for to defend
  From henceforth to our lives end!
CORRECTION: On that conditioun I am content
  To pardon you. Sen ye repent,   1890
  The Common-Weal tak by the hand
  And mak with him perpetual band!

1896 *plain*, complain; *bourd*, joke.

1909 *cleeks*, grasps.
1910 *raploch*, homespun.

1919 *rokets*, surplices.

The LORDS *and the* BURGESSES *receive* JOHN THE COMMON-
WEAL.

John, have you ony mair debates
Against my lords, the Spritual Estates?
JOHN: Na, sir, I dare nocht speak a word.
To plain on priests, it is na bourd!
BISHOP: Flyte on thy fill, fool, I defy thee,
Sa that thou shaw but the verity!
JOHN: Gramercy, then I sall not spare.
First to complain on our vicar –   1900
The poor cottar being like to die,
Havand small bairnis twa or three,
And has twa kye withouten mae,
The vicar must have ane of thae,
With the grey coat that haps the bed,
Howbeit the wife be poorly cled!
And if the wife die on the morn,
Thocht all the bairns sould be forlorn,
The other cow he cleeks away,
With the poor coat of raploch grey.   1910
Wald God this custom were put doun,
Whilk never was foundit by reasoun!
LORD: Are all thae tales true that thou tells?
POOR MAN: True, sir, the Deil stick me else!
For, by the Haily Trinity,
The same was practisit on me!
JOHN *singles out the* PARSON.
JOHN: Our parson here, he taks na other pine
But to resave his teinds and spend them syne!
POOR MAN: Our bishops, with their lusty rokets white,
They flow in riches royally and delight;   1920
Like paradise been their palaces and places,
And wants na pleasure of the fairest faces!
But doubt I wald think it a pleasant life,
Ay on, when I list, to part with my wife,
Syne tak another of far greater beauty!

1928   *like ramis . . . rage.* Allowing for poetic licence Lindsay does not exaggerate. Adam Abel, a Franciscan monk, roundly asserts in his unpublished *Rota Temporis* (in the National Library), written about 1535, that there is not one priest in Scotland fitted by his private life to preach a sermon on chastity.

1929   *unpizzlet*, rampant.

1929–30   M.

1950   *thae*, these.

1959   *weir*, war.

But ever alas, my lords, that may not be,
For I am bund, alas, in marriage,
But they like ramis rudely in their rage
Unpizzlet rins amang the silly ewes,
Sa lang as kind of nature in them grows.   1930
PARSON: Thou lies, false hureson raggit loon!
   There is na priests in all this toun
   That ever uset sic vicious crafts!
JOHN: The feind resave thae flattrand chafts!
BISHOP (*to* TEMPORALITY): My lords, why do ye thole that
        lurdan loon
   Of Kirk-men to speak sic detractioun?
   Yon villain puts me out of charity!
LORD: Why, my lord, says he ocht but verity?
   Ye can nocht stop a poor man for to plain!
BISHOP: I will not suffer sic words of yon villain!   1940
POOR MAN: Then gar give me my three fat kye again!
BISHOP: False carl, to speak to me stands thou not awe?
POOR MAN: The fiend resave them that first deviset that law!
   Within an hour efter my dad was deid
   The vicar had my cow hard by the heid!
PARSON: False hureson carl, I say that law is good,
   Because it has been lang our consuetude!
POOR MAN: When I am Pape, that law I sall put doun!
   It is a sair law for the poor commoun!
BISHOP: I mak a vow thae words thou sall repent!   1950
GOOD COUNSEL: I you require, my lords, be patient!
   We came nocht here for disputatiouns:
   We came to mak good reformatiouns!
MERCHANT: My Lords, conclude that all the temporal lands
   Be set in feu to labourers with their hands,
   With sic restrictions as sall be deviset,
   That they may live and nocht to be suppriset;
   And when they hear a proclamation,
   That the King's Grace does mak him for the weir,
   That they be ready with harness, bow and spear.   1960

1962   *corse-present* (see note to l. 1397).

1964   *kirtle*, skirt.
1965   *decern*, decree.

1970   *notar*, notary.
1970   *tak an instrument.* The Scribe, who is a notary, is to record the Bishop's protest or counter-assertion of his rights.

1974   *Et . . . tota.* The whole assembly goes along with the opinion of the majority.

1976–88 The practice of obtaining or confirming appointment to benefices by personal and often corrupt canvassing at Rome had steadily increased. One alleged effect of this costly travelling was the diminution of the already small amount of currency in this country. See note to ll. 2033–6.

1985–6 M.

1987   *Sir Simony*, presentation to a benefice in return for a material reward, money or some other gift.

1993   *cavell*, blockhead.

1995   *colourt crack*, lying tale.

GOOD COUNSEL: Sa say we all, your reason is sa good!
JOHN: What do ye of the corse-present and cow?
BISHOP: We will want nathing that we have in use,
   Kirtle nor cow, teind lamb, teind grice nor goose!
LORD: We will decern here that the Kingis grace
   Sall write unto the Papeis Haliness.
   With his consent, by proclamatioun,
   Baith corse-present and cow we sall cry doun!
BISHOP: To that, my lords, we plainly disassent!
   Notar, thereof I tak an instrument!   1970
LORD: My lord, by Him that all the warld has wrocht,
   We set nocht by wheder ye consent or nocht!
   Ye are but ane Estate and we are twa!
   Et ubi maior pars ibi tota!
JOHN: My lords, ye have richt prudently concludit!
   Tak tent now how the land is clean denudit
   Of gold and siller, whilk daily gaes to Rome
   For buds, mair than the rest of Christendom.
   Never a penny sould go to Rome at all,
   Na mair than did to Peter nor to Paul!   1980
MERCHANT: We merchants, weill I wot, within our bounds
   Has furnisht priests ten hunder thousand pounds
   For their finance; nane knaws sa weill as we!
   Therefore, my lords, devise some remedy!
   For through their pleys and their promotioun,
   Mair for deniers nor for devotioun,
   Sir Simony has made with them a band.
   The gold of weicht they lead out of the land!
GOOD COUNSEL: It is short time sen ony benefice
   Was sped in Rome, except great bishopries.   1990
   But now for an unworthy vicarage
   A priest will rin to Rome in pilgramage.
   A cavell whilk was never at the school
   Will rin to Rome and keep a bishop's mule,
   And syne come hame with mony colourt crack,
   With a burden of benefices on his back –

2013–14 M.
2013   *parochoun*, parish.
2014   *leir*, teach.

2016   *Look . . . Timothy*. Lindsay cites 1 *Timothy* iii. 1–3: 'This is a
         true saying, if a man desire the office of a bishop, he desireth
         a good work. A bishop then must be blameless, the husband
         of one wife, vigilant, sober, of good behaviour, given to
         hospitality, apt to teach; not given to wine, no striker, not
         greedy of filthy lucre, but patient, not a brawler, not
         covetous.'

2019–22 M.

2026   *teinds*, tithes.

2028   *clayis*, clothes

Whilk been against the law, ae man alane
For to possess mair benefices than ane.
Sa I conclude, my lords, and says for me
Ye sould annul all this plurality!   2000
Advise, my lords, what think ye to conclude?
LORD: Sir, by my faith, I think it very good
    That fra hencefurth na priests sall pass to Rome,
    Because our substance they do still consume.
    And als I think it best by my advice
    That ilk priest sall have but ane benefice.
GOOD COUNSEL: Mark weill, my lords, there is na benefice
    Given to a man, but for a good office!
    Wha taks office and syne they cannot use it,
    Giver and taker, I say, are baith abusit.   2010
    A bishop's office is for to be a preacher
    And of the Law of God a public teacher.
    Richt sa the Parson unto his parochoun
    Of the Evangel sould leir them a lessoun.
BISHOP: Freind, where find ye that we sould preachers be?
GOOD COUNSEL: Look what Saint Paul writes unto Timothy.
    Tak there the Book; let see if ye can spell!
    He hands Bible to BISHOP.
BISHOP: I never read that, therefore read it yoursell!
    BISHOP *casts it away.*
    Na, sir, by him that our Lord Jesus sauld,
    I read never the New Testament nor Auld,   2020
    Nor ever thinks to do sir, by the Rood!
    I hear Freirs say that reading does na good.
MERCHANT: Then before God, how can ye be excusit,
    To have an office and wots not how to use it?
    Wherefore were given you all the temporal lands,
    And all thir teinds ye have amang your hands?
    They were given you for other causes, I ween,
    Than mumble matins and hald your clayis clean!
    Ye say to the Apostles that ye succeed,
    But ye shaw nocht that into word nor deed!   2030

143

2031-4   M.

2033-6   *King David . . . King James the First.* The gift of Crown lands
by the saintly David I for the founding of bishoprics and no
less than fifteen abbeys had been noticed by John Bellenden,
in his translation (1531) of Boece's Latin history of Scotland,
as one reason for the perennial difficulties of the royal ex-
chequer: 'Thairfor the wise prince, King James the first . .
said, He was a sair Sanct for the Crown'. Lindsay's comments
on traffic in benefices and taking money out of the country
are from the same passage in Bellenden (Scottish Text
Society, vol. 2, p. 185).

2050   *tholit*, endured; *passioun*, suffering.

2061   *Sanctam Ecclesiam*, Holy Church.
2063-5   M.

POOR MAN: Sir, God nor I be stickit with a knife,
　　If ever our Parson preacht in all his life!
JOHN: What if King David were livand in thir days
　　The whilk did found sa mony gay abbeys!
　　King James the First, Roy of this regioun,
　　Said David was a sair sant to the croun.
　　I hear men say that he was something blind,
　　That gave away mair nor he left behind.
ABBOT: My lord Bishop, I mervel how that ye
　　Suffer this carl for to speak heresy!　　　　　　　2040
　　For by my faith, my lord, will ye tak tent,
　　He serves for to be brunt incontinent!
　　Ye cannot say but it is heresy,
　　To speak against our law and liberty!
　　There is a great commotion. The SPIRITUAL ESTATE *cry, 'Burn
　　him!'* CORRECTION *intervenes and addresses* JOHN.
CORRECTION: Shaw furth your faith and feignye nocht!
　　JOHN *pauses before saying his creed.*
JOHN: I believe in God that all has wrocht,
　　And create every thing of nocht;
　　And in his Son, our Lord Jesu,
　　Incarnate of the Virgin true;
　　Wha under Pilate tholit passioun,　　　　　　　2050
　　And deit for our salvatioun;
　　And on the thrid day rais again,
　　As Haly Scripture shawis plain.
　　And als, my Lord, it is weill kend,
　　How he did to the heaven ascend,
　　And set him down at the richt hand
　　Of God the Father, I understand,
　　And sall come judge on Doomesday . . .
　　What will ye mair, sir, that I say?
CORRECTION: Shaw furth the rest – this is na game!　　2060
JOHN: I trow Sanctam Ecclesiam . . .
　　But nocht in thir Bishops nor thir Freirs!
LORD: My lords, let be your disputatioun.

2065   *fra-thine*, henceforth; *disponet*, dealt with.

2070   *gormand*, greedy.

2073–4   M.

2077   *plack*, farthing.
2077   M. SCRIBE does not appear in Kemp's version. Compare other comic complaints in this play about unpaid work.

2080   *pelour*, thief.
2081   *senye*, diocesan court.
2081   M.
2082   *meir*, mare.
2083   *quarrel*, quarry.
2084   M.
2085   *meinye*, company.
2086–96   POOR MAN recites the first words of various legal styles, in parody of the law's formalities and delays: *citandum*, to be summoned; *libellandum*, the pursuer's first plea; *ad opponendum*, the defender's reply; *interloquendum*, decree before decision is given; *ad replicandum*, the pursuer's reply; *concludendum*, conclusion; *pronunciandum*, the sentence.

2092–3   M.

Conclude with firm deliberatioun
How Prelats fra-thine sall be disponet.
MERCHANT (*to* CORRECTION): I think, for me, even as ye first
    proponet,
That the King's grace sall give na benefice
But to a preacher that can use that office.
The silly saulis that been Christis sheep
Sould nocht be given to gormand wolves to keep!   2070
What been the cause of all the heresies
But the abusion of the prelacies?
They will correct and will nocht be correckit,
Thinkand to na prince they will be subjeckit.
LORD: We think your counsel is very good,
    As ye have said we all conclude!
SCRIBE: I write all day but gets never a plack!
POOR MAN: Och, my lords, for the Haly Trinity,
    Remember to reform the consistory!
PARSON: What cause has thou, false pelour, for to plainye?   2080
    Where was ye ever summont to their senye?
POOR MAN: Marry! I lent my gossip my meir to fetch hame coals
    And he her drount into the quarrel holes!
And I ran to the Consistory for to plainye,
And there I happent amang a greedy meinye.
They gave me first a thing they call *citandum*,
Within aucht days I gat but *libellandum*,
Within a month I gat *ad opponendum*,
In half a year I gat *interloquendum*,
And then I gat – how call ye it? – *ad replicandum:*   2090
But I could never a word yet understand him!
And then they gart me cast out mony placks,
And gart me pay for four and twenty Acts,
But or they came half gait to *concludendum*
The fiend a plack was left for to defend him.
Of *pronunciandum* they made me wonder fain,
But I gat never my good grey meir again!
LORD: My lords, we mon reform thir consistory laws,

147

2104–5   M.

2115   *ludging*, lodging.

2119   *the noble nuns*. Hamer reads 'innis', but 'nuns' is clearly meant. The heads of convents were often of noble family and affected a luxury much satirized.

2121   *dortour*, dormitory; *dourly*, harshly; *dang*, thrust.

2122–2170 M.

2126   *digne*, worthy.

Whase great defame above the heavens blaws,
Sa that the Kingis honour we may avance.   2100
We will conclude, as they have done in France –
Let Spritual matters pass to Sprituality,
And Temporal matters to Temporality!
BISHOP: We will not want our profit, by Sant Geil!
LORD: Your profit is against the Common Weil!
  VERITY *and* CHASTITY *now press their complaint.*
VERITY: My sovereign, I beseek your excellence,
  Use justice on Sprituality,
  The whilk to us has done great violence.
  Because we did rehearse the verity
  They put us close into captivity;   2110
  And sa remaint into subjectioun,
  Into great languor and calamnity,
  Till we were freed by King Correctioun.
CHASTITY: My lord, I have great cause for to complain,
  I could get na ludging into this land,
  The Spiritual State had me sa at disdain.
  With Dame Sensual they have made sic a band,
  Amang them all na freindship, sirs, I fand:
  And when I cam the noble nuns amang,
  My lusty Lady Prioress fra-hand,   2120
  Out of her dortour dourly she me dang!
VERITY: With the advice, Sir, of the Parliament,
  Heartly we mak you supplicatioun,
  Cause King Correctioun tak incontinent
  Of all this sort examinatioun,
  If they be digne of deprivatioun.
  My prudent Lords, I say that poor craftsmen
  Above some Prelats are mair for to commend.
CORRECTION (*to* BISHOP): Ye are a Prince of Sprituality;
  How have ye uset your office now let see.   2130
BISHOP: My Lords, when was there ony Prelats wont
  Of their office till ony King mak count?
  But of my office if ye wald have the feill,

2135   *For I tak in my count*, For I take in [collect] my rental.

2136   *ane*, one, a single; *beir*, barley.

2138   *my buttock-mail, my cotes*, my ecclesiastical fines for fornication, and my portion of the goods of the deceased to be paid for confirmation of his testament.

2143–4   *I let . . . mule*, Don't think I am a fool in respect of worldly wisdom and success just because I ride on a bishop's mule.

2148   *herriet*, pillaged (see note to 415).

2153   *Carail*, Crail, a port of east Fife.

2164   *the catch*, hand-tennis.

I let you wit I have it usit weill.
For I tak in my count twice in the year,
Wanting nocht of my teind ane boll of beir!
I gat good payment of my Temporal lands,
My buttock-mail, my cotes and my offrands.
Howbeit I dare nocht plainly spouse a wife
Yet Concubenes I have had four or five,   2140
And to my sons I have given rich rewairds,
And all my dochters marriet upon lairds.
I let you wit, my Lord, I am na fool
Forwhy I ride upon an ambland mule.
CORRECTION: I weend your office had been for to preach,
    And God's law to the people teach!
    Wherefore wear ye that mitre, ye me tell!
BISHOP: I wot nocht, man, by Him that herriet hell!
CORRECTION: Sir Scribe, ye sall, at Chastity's request,
    Pass and exame yon three in goodly haist.   2150
SCRIBE: Father Abbot, this Council bids me speir;
    How ye have uset your abbey they wald hear.
ABBOT: There is na monks fra Carrick to Carail
    That fares better and drinks mair halesome ale.
    My Prior is a man of great devotioun,
    Therefore daily he gets a double portioun.
    My paramours is baith as fat and fair
    As ony wench into the toun of Ayr.
    I send my sons to Paris to the schools,
    I traist in God that they sall be na fools!   2160
    And all my dochters I have weill providit.
    Now judge ye if my office be weill guidit!
SCRIBE: Maister Parson shaw us if ye can preach.
PARSON: Thocht I preach not I can play at the catch.

2165–70 Lindsay clearly enjoys his sporting parson. After the exam-
ination of the Prioress a learned Doctor preaches a model
sermon – too long for inclusion here – on Christian love and
its duties, and enumerates the Seven Deadly Sins. The Bishop,
Abbot and Parson, refuse to be edified, and the incredulous
and indignant Parson exclaims:

> Came doun dastart and gang sell draiff!
> I understand nocht what thou said.
> Thy words were neither corn nor caiff.
> I wald thy tongue again were laid!
> Where thou says Pride is deidly sin,
> I say Pride is but honesty,
> And Covetice of warldly win
> Is but wisdom, I say for me.
> Ire Hardiness, and Gluttony
> Is nathing else but lifeis food.
> The natural sin of Lechery
> Is but true love. All thir are good! . . .
> But were they sin, I understand
> We men of Kirk wald never use them!

2166	*ferily*, vigorously.
2167	*tables*, backgammon.
2169	*four-nookit*, four-cornered.
2171–4	Spoken by Correction in Kemp's version.
2172	*guess*, give an account.
2176	*fra-hand*, forthwith.
2179–84	M.
2185	*fleyt*, frightened.

2190	*wame*, belly.

2192	*feignyit*, feigning.

I wot there is not ane amang you all
Mair ferily can play at the football.
And for the carts, the tables and the dice,
Above all Parsons I may beir the prise.
Our round bonnets we mak them now four-nookit,
Of richt fine stuff, if ye list come and look it.   2170
SCRIBE: What say ye now, my Lady Prioress?
How have ye uset your office, can ye guess?
What was the cause ye refuset harboury
To this young lusty Lady Chastity?
PRIORESS (*haughtily*): I do my office efter auld use and wount.
To your Parliament I will mak na mair count.
CORRECTION *now points to* FLATTERY, *still in the stocks and*
disguised as a friar, and to PRIORESS.
CORRECTION: I counsel you, sir, now fra-hand
Banis yon freir out of this land.
Yon Prioress, withouten fable,
I think she is nocht profitable   2180
   For Christis regioun.
To begin reformatioun
Mak of them deprivatioun.
   This is my opinioun.
FIRST SERGEANT: Come on, sir Freir, and be nocht fleyt.
The King, our maister, mon be obeyt,
   But ye sall have na harm.
He takes FLATTERY *out of the stocks.*
If ye wald travel fra toun to toun,
I think this hood and heavy goun
   Will hald your wame owr warm.   2190
He pulls off FLATTERY'S *habit, so that the motley is revealed.*
GOOD COUNSEL: Sir, by the Haily Trinity,
This same is feignyit Flattery.
   I ken him by his face.
Believand for to get promotioun,
He said that his name was Devotioun,
   And sa beguilet your Grace.

153

2200   *pavane*, stately dance.

2204   *cow-clink*, whore.

2210   *wary*, curse.

2224   *widdiefows*, gallows-birds, here applied to the sergeants.

2229   *graith*, get ready.

The FIRST SERGEANT *now pulls the* PRIORESS *from among the*
SPIRITUAL ESTATE.
FIRST SERGEANT: Come on, my Lady Prioress,
    We sall leir you to dance,
  And that within a little space
    A new pavane of France!   2200
   The sergeants pulling off her habit show a gay dress underneath.
SECOND SERGEANT: Now, brother, by the Mess,
    By my judgment I think
  This haily Prioress
    Is turnt in a cow-clink!
PRIORESS: I give my freinds my malisoun.
  That me compellt to be a nun,
    And wald nocht let me marry!
  It was my freindis greediness
  That gart me be a Prioress.
    Now heartly I them wary!   2210
  Howbeit that Nuns sings nichts and days
  Their heart wots nocht what their mouth says,
    The sooth I you declare;
  Makand you intimatioun,
  To Christis congregatioun
    Nuns are nocht necessare.
  But I sall do the best I can
  And marry some good honest man,
    And brew good ale and tun.
  Marriage, by my opinioun,   2220
  It is better Religioun
    As to be Freir or Nun!
FLATTERY: My lords, for God's sake, let not hang me,
  Howbeit thir widdiefows wald wrang me!
    I can mak na debate
  To win my meat at pleuch nor harrows,
  But I sall help to hang my marrows,
    Baith Falset and Deceit!
CORRECTION: Than pass thy way and graith the gallows!

2235   *novelles*, news.

2251   *gragit*, excommunicated.
2252–5   M.

Syne help for to hang up thy fallows,   2230
　　Thou gets na other grace!
The gallows are brought in.
DECEIT: Now Flattery, my auld companion,
　What does yon King Correctioun?
　　Knaws thou not his intent?
　Declare to us of thy novelles!
FLATTERY: Ye'll all be hangit, I see nocht else,
　　And that incontinent!
DECEIT: Now walaway, will ye gar hang us?
　The Deil brocht yon curst King amang us,
　　For meikle sturt and strife!   2240
FLATTERY: I had been put to deid amang you,
　Were nocht I took on hand to hang you,
　　And sa I savit my life!
CORRECTION: With the advice of King Humanity,
　Here I determine with ripe advisëment,
　　That all thir prelates sall deprivit be!
KING: As ye have said, but doubt it sall be done.
　The COURTIERS *lay hands on the* PRELATES.
WANTONNESS: My lords, we pray you to be patient,
　For we will do the King's commandëment!
BISHOP: I mak a vow to God, and ye us handle   2250
　Ye sall be curst and gragit with book and candle!
　The SPIRITUAL ESTATE *is despoiled and is seen to wear motley.*
MERCHANT: We mervell of you paintit sepultures,
　That was sa bauld for to accept sic cures,
　With glorious habit ridand upon your mules.
　Now men may see ye are but very fools!
BISHOP: We say the Kings were greater fools than we,
　That us promovit to sa great dignity!
ABBOT: There is a thousand in the Kirk, but doubt,
　Sic fools as we, if they were weill socht out!
　Now brother, sen it may na better be,   2260
　Let us ga soup with Sensuality!

2264   *brether*, brothers.

2264–77   M.

2266   *lift*, sky

2273   *tocher-good*, dowry.

2279   *garmoun*, garment, gown.

2280   *owrlookit*, neglected.

2281   *crookit*, lame.

2282   *singular profit*, self-interest; *suppriset*, oppressed.

2283   *nakit*, defenceless; *disguiset*, ill-clothed.

2285   *abilyement*, dress.

2287   *Salve res publica*, Hail to the Commonwealth.

They go to SENSUALITY.

SENSUALITY: Pass fra us, fools, by Him that has us wrocht,
  Ye ludge nocht here, because I knaw you nocht!

BISHOP: I see nocht else, brether, withouten fail,
  But this false warld is turnit top owr tail.
  Sen all is vain that is under the lift,
  To win our meat we mon make other shift.
  With our labour except we mak debate,
  I dreid full sair we want baith drink and meat.

ABBOT: Allace, this reformatioun I may wary,   2270
  For I have yet twa dochters for to marry,
  And they are baith contrackit, by the Rood,
  And wots nocht now to pay their tocher-good!

PARSON: The Deil may care for this unhappy chance,
  For I am young and thinks to pass to France,
  And tak wages amang the men of weir,
  And win my living with my sword and spear.

GOOD COUNSEL (*to* CORRECTION): Or ye depart, Sir, of this
      regioun,
  Give John the Common-Weal a gay garmoun!
  Because the Common-Weal has been owrlookit,   2280
  That is the cause that Common-Weal is crookit.
  With singular profit he has been sa suppriset,
  That he is baith cauld, nakit and disguiset.

CORRECTION: As ye have said, Father, I am content.
  Sergeants, give John a new abilyement
  Of satin, damas, or of the velvet fine,
  And give him place into our Parliament syne!

Music. They clothe JOHN *gorgeously and receive him into Parliament. The* ESTATES *sing* 'Salve, res publica.'

POOR MAN: I give you my braid benison,
  That has given Common-Weal a goun;
  But I beseek you, for All Hallows,   2290
  Cause hang Deceit and all his fallows,
  And banis Flattery of the toun,
  For there was never sic a loon!

2294	*by the gait*, out of the way.
2294–314	were spoken in the play at Common Theft's first entrance, before the examination of the clergy, in a scene in which Public Oppression, a typical protector of reivers, betrays him, leaving him in the stocks. The scene interrupts the main action but has been omitted chiefly for want of space.
2294–2347	M. Theft does not appear in Kemp's version.
2295	*thrang*, crowd.
2309	*forlorn*, undone.
2311	*craig*, neck.
2316	*sweir*, loath.
2318	*widdy*, gallows rope.
2322	*limmer*, bold rascal.
2324	*tippet*, a cape fastened round the neck. Hamer and Kinsley in their editions simply translate 'hangman's rope'.
2325	*a fellon rippet*, a great ado. It was from Lindsay that Allan Ramsay learned the trick of writing semi-comic 'last dying speeches'.

THEFT *enters running and finds* POOR MAN *in his way.*

THEFT: Ga by the gait man, let me gang!
  How Deil cam I into this thrang?
  With sorrow I may sing my sang
    And I be tane,
  For I have run baith nicht and day.
  Through speed of foot I gat away.
  If I be kend here, wallaway,   2300
    I will be slain!
POOR MAN: What is thy name man, by thy thrift?
THEFT: Hureson, they call me Common Thift,
  Forwhy I had na other shift
    Sen I was born!
  In Ewesdale was my dwelling place.
  Mony a wife gart I cry alace.
  At my hand they gat never grace,
    But ay forlorn.
  Get this curst King me in his grips   2310
  My craig will wit what weighs my hips.
  The Deil I give his tongue and lips
    That of me tells!
  Adieu, I dare na langer tarry.
  The FIRST SERGEANT *recognizes and seizes* THEFT.
FIRST SERGEANT: Come here, sir Theif, come here, come here!
  When was ye wont to be sa sweir?
  To hunt cattle ye were ay speedy,
  Therefore ye sall wave in a widdy.
THEFT: Mon I be hangit? Allace, allace!
  Is there nane here may get me grace?   2320
  Yet or I die give me a drink.
FIRST SERGEANT: Thou art a limmer, I stand ford!
  Slip in thy heid into this cord,
  For thou had never a meeter tippet!
THEFT: Allace, this is a fellon rippet!
  Repent your lives ye plain oppressours,
  All ye misdoers and transgressours,

L   161

2329 *mak you ford*, prepare yourselves.

2334–44 Common Theft lists the main reiving families of the West Border.

2343 *slicht*, skilful.

2346 *fangit*, caught.

2351 *mangit*, mad.

2360 *ill-deedy*, evil-doing

Or else gar choose you good confessours,
 And mak you ford.
For if ye tarry in this land   2330
And come under Correctioun's hand,
Your grace sall be, I understand,
 A good sharp cord.
Adieu my brethren common thieves,
That helpit me in my mischieves.
Adieu Grosars, Nicksons and Bells,
Oft have we faren out-through the fells.
Adieu Robsons, Hawes and Pyles,
That in our craft has mony wiles,
Littles, Trumbels and Armistrangs.   2340
Adieu all thieves that me belangs,
Tailors, Irwins and Elwands,
Speedy of foot and slicht of hands,
The Scotts of Ewesdale, and the Graemes –
I have na time to tell your names.
With King Correctioun and ye be fangit,
Beleive richt weill ye will be hangit!
THEFT *is hanged to a roll of drums. Then the* SERGEANTS *take*
DECEIT *and* FALSET *from the stocks and lead them to the gallows,*
where each makes his speech and is hanged with the same ceremony.
FIRST SERGEANT: Come here, Deceit, my companyoun!
 Saw ever man liker a loon
  To hing upon a gallows!   2350
DECEIT: This is eneuch to mak me mangit!
 Dule fell me that I mon be hangit!
  Let me speak with my fallows!
I trow wan-fortune brocht me here.
What meikle fiend made me so speedy?
Sen it was said it is seven year,
That I sould wave into a widdy.
I learit my maisters to be greedy.
Adieu, for I see na remede.
Look what it is to be ill-deedy!   2360

2363	*ye hurt my craig*, a common hanging jest.
2364	*wed*, wager; *plack*, farthing.
2365	*knag*, knot.

| 2373 | *upalands*, country. |

| 2378 | *rounand*, whispering. |

2387	*good cheap*, at a bargain price.
2388	*saip*, soap.
2389	*oyldolly*, olive oil.
2390	*ocker*, usury.

| 2392 | *double-mail*, the 'herild horse' or similar rent in kind mentioned earlier by Poor Man, which might be repeated on the death of the deceased man's widow. |
| 2393 | *ell-wand*, the rod for measuring the Scots ell, which was approximately 37 inches. |

FIRST SERGEANT: Now in this halter slip thy heid!
  Stand still! Me think ye draw aback!
DECEIT: Alas, maister, ye hurt my craig!
FIRST SERGEANT: It will hurt better, I wed a plack,
  Richt now when ye hing on a knag!
DECEIT: Adieu, my maisters, merchant men,
  I have you servit, as ye ken,
    Truly, baith air and late!
  I say to you, for conclusioun,
  I dreid ye gang to confusioun,   2370
    Fra time ye want Deceit.
  I learit you merchants mony a wile,
  The upalands wives for to beguile
    Upon a market day;
  And mak them trow your stuff was good,
  When it was rotten, by the Rood,
    And sweir it was not sa!
  I was aye rounand in your ear,
  And learit you for to ban and sweir
    What your gear cost in France,   2380
  Howbeit the Deil a word was true!
  Your craft if King Correctioun knew,
    Wald turn you to mischance!
  I learit you wiles monifauld –
  To mix the new wine with the auld,
    That fashion was na folly!
  To sell richt dear and buy good cheap,
  And mix rye-meal amang the saip,
    And saffron with oyldolly.
  Foryet nocht ocker, I counsel you,   2390
  Mair than the Vicar does the cow,
    Or lords their double-mail.
  Howbeit your ell-wand be too scant,
  Or your pound weicht three ounces want,
    Think that but little fail!
  Ye young merchants may cry alace!

2400   *perqueir*, thoroughly.

2402   *mense*, grace.

2404   *cankert*, depraved.

2410   *cummer*, trouble.

2414   *webster*, weaver.
2415   *walker*, fuller.

2426   *lorimers*, makers of bits, spurs, metal mountings for bridles and saddles.
2427   *cordiners*, cordwainers.

For wanting of your wonted grace,
    Yon curst King ye may ban!
Had I livit but half a year,
I sould have learit you crafts perqueir   2400
    To beguile wife and man!
SECOND SERGEANT: Come here, Falset, and mense the gallows!
  Ye mon hing up amang your fallows
    For your cankert conditioun!
Mony a true man have ye wrangit,
Therefore but doubt ye sall be hangit,
    But mercy or remissioun!
FALSET: Alace, mon I be hangit too?
What meikle Deil is this ado?
    How cam I to this cummer?   2410
My good maisters, ye craftismen,
Want ye Falset, full weill I ken
    Ye will all die for hunger.
Find me a Webster that is leal,
Or a Walker that will not steal!
    Their craftiness I ken.
Or a Miller that has na fault,
That will neither steal meal nor malt –
    Hald them for haily men!
At our Fleshers tak ye na grief,   2420
Thocht they blaw lean mutton and beef,
    That they seem fat and fair.
Adieu, my maisters, Wrichts and Masons,
I need not lear you ony lessons,
    Ye knaw my craft perqueir!
Adieu, Blacksmiths and Lorimers,
Adieu, ye crafty Cordiners,
    That sells the shoon owr dear!
Amang craftsmen it is a wonder
To find ten leal amang a hunder,   2430
    The truth I to you tell!
Adieu, I may na longer tarry,

2433   *the King of Fairy*, the Devil.

2435-46   M.

2440   *pin*, peg.

2443   *my father brother*. Deceit was the brother of Satan, the 'father of lies', i.e. of 'Falset'.

2444   *silly*, helpless.

2447   *wend*, gone.

2449   Hamer asks why Flattery is not hanged with the others and suggests that it was because he was a cleric, Lindsay not wishing to incur a charge of heresy or suspicion that he wanted reformation on the drastic English model; but he first enters the play as a Fool or Vice and is later only a pretended Friar. He is needed to end the proper business of the play, which has been an exposure of folly in all three Estates, and to remind the audience that folly is still very much with them. In case the point should be missed, Lindsay's production closes with an 'epilogue – interlude' in which 'Foly' himself reviews farcically all the themes of the play and chooses as his text, 'The number of fools is infinite'. Such a 'sermon joyeux' Hamer notes, 'was characteristic of the French *sottie*' or fool-play. I have omitted this post-script for its length and comparative superfluousness.

2458-67   M. The last lines given to Flattery by Kemp were these:
Mark weel! my feres the piper pay,
But Flatterie slips clean away,
     O aa the world I'm free!

2461   *scaplary*, 'scapulary', a monk's garment covering breast and back.

2462   *genners*, engenders.

2463   *black or blue*, whatever the colour or Order.

I mon pass to the King of Fairy,
   Or else straichtway to hell!
Here he looks up at his hanged companions.
Waes me for thee, good Common Thift!
Was never man made mair honest shift
   His living for to win!
There was nocht in all Liddesdale
That kye mair craftily could steal –
   Where thou hings on that pin!   2440
Sathan resave thy saul, Deceit,
Thou was to me a faithful mate,
   And als my father brother!
Dule fell the silly merchant men!
To mak them service, weill I ken
   They'll ne'er get sic another!
Fareweill, for I am to the widdy wend,
For-why Falset made never a better end!
FLATTERY: Have I not chapet the widdy weill?
   Yea, that I have, by sweet Sant Geill!   2450
   For I had nocht been wrangit,
Because I servit, by All Hallows,
To have been marshallt with my fallows,
   And heich above them hangit!
I made far mair faults nor my mates,
I beguilet all the Three Estates
   With my hypocrisy.
When I had on my freiris hood
All men believit that I was good.
   Now judge ye if I be.   2460
I knaw that cowl and scaplary
Genners mair heat nor charity,
   Thocht they be black or blue.
What haliness is there within
A wolf cled in a wether's skin?
   Judge ye if this be true.

2477   *brawl*, a lively dance tune.
2478   *hobbles*, capers.

2480   *or ever I stent*, without stopping.

Music.

DILIGENCE: Famous people, heartly I you require
    This little sport to tak in patience.
    We traist in God, live we another year,
    Where we have failit, we sall do diligence,   2470
    With mair pleasure to mak you recompense;
    Because we have been some part tedious,
    With matter rude, denude of eloquence,
    Likewise, perchance, to some men odious.
    Now let ilk man his way advance!
    Let some ga drink, and some ga dance!
    Minstrels, blaw up a brawl of France!
      Let see wha hobbles best!
    For I will rin incontinent
    To the tavern or ever I stent!   2480
    I pray to God omnipotent,
    To send you all good rest!
Music. A dance, followed by a march, during which EXEUNT
OMNES.

THE END